부전
글로컬비전센터
열리다.

이은석 지음.

OPEN. BGVC

BUJEON GLOCAL VISION CENTER

P:.

나의 하나님이여 이제 이곳에서 하는 기도에 눈을 드시고 귀를 기울이소서 (역대하 6:40)

'Now, my God, may your eyes be open and your ears attentive to the prayers offered in this place (2 Chronicles 6:40)

Contents.

OPEN. BGVC

Contents.

OPEN. BGVC

들린 볼륨,
열린 길 그리고 나눔

이은석
건축가, 아뜰리에 코마 대표

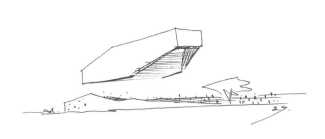

듦

문들아 너희 머리를 들지어다 영원한 문들아 들릴지어다
영광의 왕이 들어가시리로다 [시편 24:7]

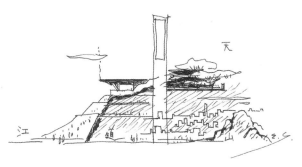

길

예수께서 이르시되 내가 곧 길이요 진리요 생명이니
나로 말미암지 않고는 아버지께로 올 자가 없느니라
[요한복음 14:6]

초월적 신성(divinity)을 물리적 구조물로 표현하려는 의지가 고딕의 수직 마천루에서 드러나듯이, 압도하는 권위를 얻기 위해서 기념비 건축은 거대 스케일과 대칭성 그리고 축성(軸性)의 형식을 따랐다. 그러나 현대적 기념성은 중력을 거스르면서 들어 올린 구조체와 수평성으로 가볍게 표현된다. 건물을 들어서 막힌 벽을 넘어 안팎을 소통하며, 이웃을 내부로 적극 초대한다. 이처럼 들린 볼륨은 기념적이지만 환대하는 건축적 자세이어서 저층부를 관통하는 실내 가로, 카페와 식당, 도서관과 같은 교회 내 상업시설에 정당성을 부여한다. 교회가 인습과 종교적 자만심을 허물면서 즐겨 이웃을 맞이할 때 그 가치는 극대화된다.

길은 구도자의 삶을 돕는다. 성서에서도 생명인 진리의 길은 곧 그리스도라 증거한다. 소통과 교류가 길 위에서 발생하는 것은 그것이 소중한 목적지로 도달하는 과정이기 때문이다. 2011년 설명회부터 2016년의 준공과 건설의 자취를 기록한 2017년 겨울에 이르기까지 7년간을 당선자로, 설계자로, 감리자로 또한 기록자로서 서울과 부산 사이의 길을 수백 번 오르내렸을 것이다. 서울과 부산을 연결하는 길도 여럿 있다. 이 길의 존재가 부전글로컬비전센터를 완성한 셈이다. 이처럼 길은 소통이고 역동이며, 새로운 세계를 향해 열린 가치이다. 그러므로 건축과 도시를 관계 짓는 실내 가로와 건물 전체를 휘감아 오르는 계단 길은 진리를 전하는 강력한 도구이며, 이 건축물이 존재하는 한 쉼 없이 작동해야 하는 핵심 동력이다.

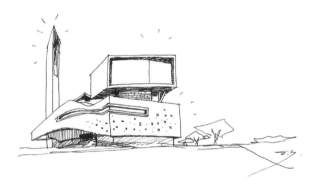

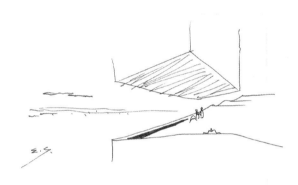

빛

너희는 세상의 빛이라 산 위에 있는 동네가 숨겨지지
못할 것이요 사람이 등불을 켜서 말 아래에 두지 아니하고
등경 위에 두나니 이러므로 집 안 모든 사람에게 비치느니라
(마태복음 5:14-15)

쉼

수고하고 무거운 짐 진 자들아 다 내게로 오라
내가 너희를 쉬게 하리라 (마태복음 11:28)

마치 부산 바다의 등대처럼 수직과 수평의 빛기둥은
이 건축물을 밝게 관통하고 있다. 그리고 곳곳에 적용한 자연
채광은 공간을 경제적으로 밝혀주기도 하지만 하늘로부터 공급
되는 빛은 아름다운 신앙적 의미도 내포한다. 오히려 가장 직설
적이면서도 자연스럽게 하늘의 은총을 드러내는 표현이며 이를
바라보는 성도들이 세상의 빛이 되어야겠다고 깨우치게 하는 상
징적 건축 언어이다. 오늘날의 건축은 날이 어두워진 도심지에
서 밖으로 새어 나오는 인공광 효과도 소홀히 하면 안 된다. 베
드로가 새벽녘 바다에서 끌어올린 물고기의 숫자와 맞춘 153개
벽면의 작은 창들은, 별빛처럼 교회 건축 역사에서 매우 이례적
이고 현대적인 상징으로 반짝인다. 마치 "내 어린양을 먹이라"라
고 말하듯이……

시내 광야의 구름 기둥처럼, 마치 거대한 파라솔처럼
이 건물 곳곳의 캐노피 아래 테라스는 자연스럽게 도시민의 피
난처로 조성하였다. 온천천의 녹지와 산책로에서부터 이어지는
외부 계단은 테라스와 공중정원들을 연결 짓고, 마침내 누하 진
입을 통해 탁 트인 옥상정원과 십자가 탑 아래에 이른다. 수평
으로 길게 뚫린 전망대를 통해 파노라믹하게 펼쳐지는 부산시
의 전경을 바라보노라면 유람선 갑판에 올라온 듯하다. 도심 한
가운데 떠 있는 거대한 배와 같이, 고난의 멍에 가득한 현세로
부터 쉼과 평강을 누릴 수 있는 하늘나라로 우리를 실어다 줄
현대적 방주요, 카테드랄(Cathedral)이다.

Prologue.

들린 볼륨, 열린 길 그리고 나눔
Lifted Volumes, Open Pathways and Sharing

014

이은석
건축가, 아뜰리에 코마 대표
Lee Eun-seok.
Architect, Atelier KOMA

숨

내가 산을 향하여 눈을 들리라 나의 도움이 어디서 올까
나의 도움은 천지를 지으신 여호와에게서로다 [시편 121:1-2]

참

오직 성령의 열매는 사랑과 희락과 화평과 오래 참음과
자비와 양선과 충성과 온유와 절제니
이같은 것을 금지할 법이 없느니라 [갈라디아서 5:22-23]

　　　　하늘을 향해 열린 전경은 하나님 사랑을, 땅을 향해 트인 숨구멍은 이웃 사랑을 의미하는 건축적 장치이다. 우리는 광장에 서서 수직의 탑을 따라 앙망하며 푸른 하늘로 열린 창, 그 거대한 캐노피 속으로 날아오르고 싶은 환희를 누린다. 위압감이 아니라 가볍게 들린 콘크리트 볼륨을 관통하며 중력을 거스르며 솟아오르는 고유의 상승감은 이 건축만의 풍요이다. 그처럼 하늘로부터 위대한 도움은 온다고 시인은 노래한다. 그리고 예배동과 교육동 사이 전 층에 걸친 중정의 숨통으로 자연광과 쾌적한 공기는 각층을 관통하며, 선큰은 땅속 깊숙한 곳 어린이 교육 공간까지 밝은 빛을 공급한다.

　　　　노출 콘크리트로 된 건축물의 가치는 견고함과 경제성 그리고 진실성에 있다. 거푸집을 걷어낸 후, 골조가 드러내는 모습을 그대로 건축물의 외관으로 수용하려는 미학적 태도이다. 그 진실성은 기독교적 삶의 윤리와 일맥상통한다. 콘크리트 마감은 날것이며, 불필요한 장식이 배제되고 형과 색과 소모적 건축행위를 절제한 미니멈의 이미지로 드러난다. 참되고 신실한 것은 화려한 안목의 정욕과 이생의 자랑은 버리고, 더 나은 하늘의 가치를 추구하려는 기독 공동체의 기본 철학이다. 그래서 노출 콘크리트는 근검절약의 정서를 상징하는 개신교적 건축재료이다. 마감 재료를 결정하는 과정이 그리 순탄치는 않았으나, 경제성과 진실성을 획득하기 위해 더 나은 선택을 하였다. 견고한 노출 콘크리트 구조체는 바로 순수하고 진지한 기독 신앙의 은유인 것이다.

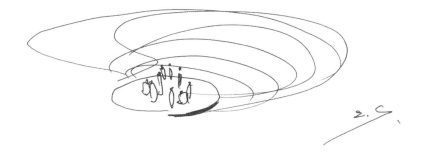

모임

모이기를 폐하는 어떤 사람들의 습관과 같이 하지 말고
오직 권하여 그 날이 가까움을 볼수록 더욱 그리하자
(히브리서 10:25)

　　　　부전글로컬비전센터의 가장 우선적 가치는 모이는 공
간 조성에 있다. 모이는 일은 그 자체로 그리스도인들 예배의 중
요한 행위이므로 곳곳에 크고 작은 모임의 장소를 다양하게 펼
쳐놓고, 수많은 모임을 배려하고 있다. 체육관부터 공연장, 예식
홀, 음악당, 교육실, 전시실과 스카이라운지 그리고 작은 세미나
실부터 수천 명이 운집하는 대집회실과 옥외 집회공간에 이르
기까지 각기 특성에 따라 다채로운 기능을 조성했다. 집회 장소
들을 유기적으로 연결하기 위한 설계 방식도 동원되었는데, 특
히 공항이나 철도 역사처럼 넉넉한 콘코스(concours)를 모임 공
간 사이에 배치하여, 함께 모이고 머무르고 나누면서 풍족한 삶
을 누리게 하였다. 말씀과 찬양과 교제의 잔치들, 성서에서 소
개하는 하늘나라의 모습도 이처럼 모임의 잔치가 아니던가!

Lifted Volumes, Open Pathways and Sharing

Lee Eun-seok.
Architect,
Atelier KOMA

Lifting

Lift up your heads, O you gates; be lifted up, you ancient doors, that the King of glory may come in. (Psalms 24:7)

Monumental architecture used to have to adopt a grand scale, symmetry, and a strong axis to gain an overwhelming authority, as exhibited by the willingness to express transcendental divinity in the tall spires and structures of the Gothic period. However, today monumentality is expressed lightly by a structure that appears to levitate and exist apart from gravity and horizontality. A lifted building can communicate inside and outside across a wall and invite neighbours into the interior. This lifted volume appears monumental but welcoming in terms of architecture, and this justifies commercial facilities such as an indoor street penetrating the lower part, cafes, restaurants and a library. When a church welcomes its neighbours by giving up conventions or religious rigidity, its value can be maximised.

Way

Jesus answered, "I am the way and the truth and the life. No one comes to the Father except through me." (John 14:6)

A way helps us lead the life of a truth-seeker. It is written in the Bible that the way of truth and life is Christ. This way facilitates communication and exchange because it is a process of enquiry leading to the precious destination. I have traveled back and forth between Seoul and Busan hundreds of times as a competition winner, architect, supervisor and recorder, ever since the briefing session in 2011, the completion of construction in 2016, and in the winter of 2017 when I recorded the history of the construction. Seoul and Busan are also connected by many routes, which helped complete the Bujeon Glocal Vision Center. In this way, a path becomes a dynamic communication line, and a value open to the new world. Therefore, an indoor street that links the church to the city, and a stairway that surrounds the whole building both become powerful tools to convey truth and key driving forces that work as long as the church exists.

Light

You are the light of the world. A city on a hill cannot be hidden. Neither do people light a lamp and put it under a bowl. Instead they put it on its stand, and it gives light to everyone in the house. (Matthew 5:14-15)

Just like the lighthouse of the sea in front of Busan, bright columns of vertical and horizontal light penetrate this building. Natural lighting here and there also contributes to the maintenance cost savings, and the light that comes from the sky has a beautiful religious meaning. It expresses the heavenly grace in the most direct and natural way, and plays a role in a symbolic architectural language that teaches believers to act as the light of the world. That said, today architecture should not neglect the effects of artificial light emitted by the downtown area long after sunset. The 153 small windows on the wall, which stand for the number of fish St. Peter pulled out of the sea at dawn, glitter like stars and act as very unusual, modern symbols in the history of church architecture. They seem to say, 'Feed my lamb'.

Rest

Come to me, all you who are weary and burdened, and I will give you rest. (Matthew 11:28)

Terraces under the canopies all around this building naturally create refuges for the public like a giant parasol or like a cloud pillar in a downtown wilderness. The outer stairway, which begins at the green and promenade along the Oncheon Stream, connects the terraces with the hanging gardens and finally leads to the open roof garden and the cross tower (by entering through the entrance under the upper floor). Observing the panoramic view of Busan spreading out before you from a horizontal observation deck may make you feel as if you are on the deck of a cruise ship. The church, like a huge ship floating at the centre of the city, is a kind of modern Noah's ark and cathedral, which will bring us to the kingdom of heaven where we can take a rest and enjoy a realm of peace freed from this painful life.

Breath

I lift up my eyes to the hills - where does my help come from? My help comes from the LORD, the Maker of heaven and earth. (Psalms 121:1-2)

In terms of architectural devices, an open view towards the sky implies love shown for God, and a windpipe towards the earth reveals love towards our neighbours. Standing in the square and looking up to the vertical tower, we can relish the joy of flying up into the blue sky through an open window and into the huge canopy. The unique sense of soaring up against the forces of gravity which penetrate the lifted concrete volume appear not domineering but rich, found only in this building. A poet once sang that great help comes from the Heavens. The courtyard is between a worshipping place and an educational hall, and it is open to all floors, which enables natural light and fresh air to reach each floor. The sunken area plays a role in supplying natural light to the children's classrooms in the basement.

Truth

But the fruit of the Spirit is love, joy, peace, patience, kindness, goodness, faithfulness, gentleness and self-control. Against such things there is no law. (Galatians 5:22-23)

The value of the exposed concrete building lies in its durability, economic feasibility and authenticity. It is an aesthetic attitude to accept an appearance defined by the frame as the appearance of the building after removing the form works. The authenticity is in accord with the ethics of Christian life. Concrete finishing is expressed by a minimal image that excludes unnecessary decoration and abstains from shape, colour, and exhaustive building practices. Truth and sincerity is the basic philosophy of the Christian community, guided by a commitment to abandon the lust of the flesh, the lust of the eyes, the pride of life and to pursue the better values communicated by Heaven. Thus, exposed concrete is a building material fit for a Protestant idea that symbolises thrift and saving. The process of determining the finishing materials didn't go smoothly, but we made a better choice to secure economic feasibility and authenticity. Therefore, this robust structure of exposed concrete is a metaphor for the pure and serious Christian faith.

Gathering

Let us not give up meeting together, as some are in the habit of doing, but let us encourage one another - and all the more as you see the Day approaching. (Hebrews 10:25)

The primary value of the Glocal Vision Center depends on how to create a gathering space. Gathering itself is an important part of Christian worship, so various places have been planned for large and small gatherings here and there. They have various functions ranging from the gymnasium to the performance hall, courtesy hall, music hall, education room, exhibition room, sky lounge, small seminar room, large conference hall and outdoor meeting space. They are designed according to their characteristics, with thousands of occupants in mind. In addition, a method to link the meeting places was applied organically, and, most of all, a large concourse like that of airport or railway station has been placed between the meeting spaces, which helps the believers to enrich their lives as they gather, stay and share. Aren't the feasts of gospel, praise, and friendship, and the kingdom of heaven described in the Bible, also that of such a gathering?

이은석
건축가, 아뜰리에 코마 대표
Lee Eun-seok,
Architect, Atelier KOMA

종교를 위한
건축적 알레고리

박길룡
국민대학교 건축대학
명예교수

부전교회 가는 길

부산역에 내려, 택시를 타고 기사에게 부전교회에 간다고 했지만, 위치를 어떻게 설명해야 할지 막연했다. 쓸데없는 걱정이었다. 차가 출발하고 운전기사는 자기가 아는 이 교회의 이야기를 풀어놓기 시작했다. 그 땅이 옛날 송월타월의 공장이었다든지, 땅 주인이 교회를 위해 대지를 대단히 싼값에 공여했다든지, 시공자가 공사비를 엄청 깎아 주어 건축할 수 있었다든지…. 놀랍다.

다시 말해 '부전교회'는 부산 시민에게(이 택시기사가 교회 신자였는지는 모르겠지만) 일반 명사이며 상식인 것이다. 부산은 대도시이니 시골 마을교회와 다를 것이고, 부전교회가 아직 세계유산의 존재도 아니다. 아마 시각적 전모가 잘 드러나는 위치에서 건축이 힘껏 모뉴멘탈하기 때문일지 모른다. 교회가 워낙 부산에서 오랜 전통으로 덕을 쌓아 왔는지도 모르겠다. 여하튼 중요한 것은 이 시대에도 교회는 대단히 사회적이라는 것이다. 택시기사의 오리엔테이션 덕분에 훨씬 이해를 단축할 수 있었다.

현대 – 도시 – 교회 – 당

이 글을 쓰는 사람은 무종교자이지만, 세계건축사를 연구하면서 수많은 교회를 만났다. 세계문화사를 빛내는 존재로서 종교 건축은 동서양을 막론하고 시대사의 중심임을 잘 안다. 필자는 (믿는 종교가 없다고 계속 변명) 교회당에 들어서면 모자를 벗고, 사찰에 들어서면 몸을 단정히 한다. 장소에는 혼이 있고, 그곳이 신의 장소라면, 우리 일상을 초월하는 공간이라고 믿기 때문이다. 그렇지만 안타깝게도 모든 교회당이 장소의 혼을 가진

것은 아니다.

종교의 세속화와 함께 신의 존재감이 휘발된 교회당이 많다. 자본에 휘둘리는 교회도 보고, 권력의 수단이 되는 것은 더 분명히 보인다. 그러나 여전히 우리 사회에서 은혜의 공간, 영적인 장소를 가지고 있기에 문화가 유지된다고 믿는다. 그러면 교회에서 장소의 혼은 어떻게 알아보나.

일반적으로는 종교적 알레고리로 통한다. 그래서 감히 말하건대, 건축가는 그 믿음의 메신저라고 생각한다. 고딕의 날카로움이 르네상스에 이르러 어떻게 순화되는지, 문예부흥이 인본주의를 기반으로 하지만 교황권이 극단에 이르는 후기 르네상스에서 가톨릭의 모순, 기독교의 세계화와 선교의 역사, 피가 흥건했던 종교개혁과 바꾼 개신, 특히 우리나라 근대화의 필연이었던 기독교는 특별하다고 생각한다. 그리고 그 모두가 건축역사에 복제되어 있다.

조선 선교의 피 터 위에 교회당을 세웠고, 문화적 충돌에도 불구하고 대중을 계몽하며, 봉건에 가려졌던 인본과 사랑을 알려주었다. 조선에서 교회당은 사람들의 사건이었으며, 서구 문화의 창구였던 것을 기억한다. 독립운동도 지원하였다. 벽돌로 건축하는 법, 뾰족하게 높이 짓는 법, 회중이 모이는 공간을 처음 알았다. 커뮤니티를 인식하고, 여성과 아동, 사랑과 계몽과 민주로 사회문화의 큰 줄기를 더하였다.

현대에 들어 한국 기독교는 (그 특별한 사회적 의미 때문에) 급팽창하고, 종교학과가 많아지고 목회자를 양산한다. 그러면서 교회 건축은 '너무 많은 것들' 중 하나가 되었다. 그것이 종교적 대중화라는 명분으로 건축문화를 허접스럽게 하고 있는지도 안다. 이제 한국의 현대 교회 건축은 건축적 무지들(훨씬 지

1 —— 「아름다운 교회 건축」, 두란노(2008)
「Buautiful Church Architecture」, Duranno(2008)

2 —— 온천천에서 바라본 부전글로컬비전센터
scenery from Oncheoncheon,
Bujeon Glocal Vision Center

©Choi Sang Dong

1

2

배적인)과 정화된 의식(소수이지만 빛나는)을 구분한다. 양식적 오만과 편견, 상징의 과잉, 몸집에 집착하는 반사회성이 무지의 세계이다. 반면에 양식적 겸손, 검소한 상징, 친화적 커뮤니티, 정화된 건축을 구분한다.

이제 한 종교의 주변 자가 교회당 건축을 보려는 입장이 어느 정도 정리된 듯하다.

교수 건축가

건축가 이은석은 대학교수이다. 교수 건축가는 일반 건축가와 구분되는 행태가 있는데, 끊임없이 건축을 방법화하고 논리화한다. 이은석 교수가 이지적 건축가임은 그의 저서들이 인증한다. 『새로운 교회 건축 이렇게 하라』(두란노, 2001)는 조금 방자한 뜻 같으나, 한국의 교회 건축문화를 (오죽 답답했으면) 직설적으로 말한다. 『아름다운 교회 건축』(두란노, 2008)에서 '아름답다'는 것은 예쁜 모습이 아니라, 진정성의 미학이다. 그래서 이 건축가는 형찰적 투지를 가지고 있다. 가끔 비타협적이거나, 명분이 뚜렷해야 물러설 줄도 안다.

교수 건축가로서 또는 건축가 교수라고 하여 건축 수행에서 더 수월한 조건에 있는 것은 아니다. 가끔 그에게 논리가 자유를 압박하거나, 원리가 자의를 제약하는 경우를 본다. 하지 말아야 할 것을 규정하는 것은 단정한 자기를 위해 당연하지만, 뭘 하지 말아야 하는지는 해야 할 것만큼이나 어려운 사실이다. 그래서 그의 '아름다움'에는 억제된 욕망이 있다. 그것이 분방할 일을 제어하지만 또한 스스로를 제약하는 가름이 된다.

대형 교회와 공간 프로그램

너른 하늘을 보기 위해 얼마나 너른 땅이 필요한가. 대형 교회의 패러다임은 세계가 고민하는 과제이다. 크게 보면 교회당은 교회의 포장인데, 무엇을 품는가는 목회의 개념이다. 그래서 많은 것을 크게 담고 싶으면 대형 교회가 된다. 현대사회에서 거대 교회의 개연성을 이해하지만, 욕망에 흐린 목회를 알기 때문에 잘 가려 볼 일이다. 교회 세습, 경영 분규, CEO형 담임 등을 대중들도 들어서 알고 있다.

최근 교회 프로그래밍에서 커뮤니티 활동을 적극적으로 확장하는 경향이다. 현대의 새로운 신자 세대가 만드는 문화구조이겠지만, 환경이 문화를 만든다는 환경결정론도 있다. 커서 더 많은 것을 하겠지만, 거대 교회가 불편한 것은 그들의 위압적 크기가 종교적이지 않은 경우를 자주 보기 때문이다. 순수한 공간의 크기는 지각 거리로 결정되는데 시각, 청각, 느낌 공간감 등이 결정하는 크기이다. 현대 교회가 커지면서 마이크로 확성하고 프로젝션으로 확대하는 일이 불편해 보인다. 회중석 규모가 3,000석이라면 콘서트홀로서도 큰 공간이다. 세종문화회관이 당초 4,500석에서 3,000석으로 줄였고, 예술의 전당 콘서트홀이 2,500석이다. 음악당을 아무리 크게 짓고 싶어도 음향상의 임계 규모가 있다. 보통 확성기를 쓰지 않고 음악을 전달할 수 있는 최적 스케일을 1,500석 정도로 말하여진다.

교회도 마찬가지여서 큰 예배공간에서는 경(經)에 집중하기 어렵고, 강론을 소리로만 듣는 것 같다. 이 부족성을 보충하기 위해 예배가 쇼나 이벤트처럼 된다. 규모가 커지면 2층 회중석을 두는데 이게 더 문제다. 예배를 참여하는 것이 아니고 관람하는 공간이 되는 것이다.

종교를 위한 건축적 알레고리
Architectural Allegory for Religion

박길룡
국민대학교 건축대학 명예교수
Park, Kil-young.
Emeritus Professor, School of Architecture
Kookmin University

1

2

부전교회는 3,000석 규모인데 공간 형식으로 반원 아레나 형식을 취했다. 부채살형 평면은 구심형으로서 성단으로의 집중력도 좋다. 2층 발코니를 만들지 않고 한 층에서 예배를 공유할 수 있는 행태 디자인이 보인다.

건축적 알레고리

건축이 말을 하고, 뜻을 전달할 수 있다는 믿음에 건축가는 상징·수사를 표현에 얹기 시작한다. 아마 그 극치가 고딕 성당이었을 것이다. 그러나 르네상스가 도래하며 사실상 상징성을 버렸다. 다시 바로크가 수사를 확장하면서 건축을 극적으로 만드는 버릇이 생겼다. 모더니즘은 모든 의미, 상징을 벗어버리지만, 후기 모더니즘에서 건축적 수사가 회복하는 것 같다. 다만 그 상징과 수사는 추상화되고 은유로 작동한다.

문학건축처럼 상징(symbolism) − 메타포(metaphor) − 알레고리(allegory)로 말하자면 단계가 있어 보인다. 중세 고딕에서 교회는 온몸이 상징체였다. 몸(성신), 빛(성심), 십자가(성자)가 종교심을 상징한다. 이에 더하여 성물, 성화, 아이콘이 상징을 지원하였다. 메타포는 상징과 달리 꼭 그렇게 보이지만은 않지만, 그럴듯하다는 뜻으로 안다. 문학이 직설적 사실만을 말할 수 없기에 은유는 언어의 생명이다. 건축도 마찬가지다. 알레고리는 좀 더 느슨하다. 사람마다 달리 느낄 수 있는 여지가 넓으며, 작가에게는 보다 폭넓은 문학적 개진이 가능해진다.

이은석의 건축은 건축적 상징이건, 구체적인 수사이건, 하고 싶은 말이 있다. 다만 그의 언어는 다분히 추상적이고 은유적이기 때문에 우리는 새겨들어야 한다. 다음과 같은 것을 읽었다.

크기의 조형

보통 크기 자체가 미학일 때도 있다. 작아서 아름다움도 있고 큰 규모의 미적 쾌감이 있다. 큰 것은 스펙터클한 시각적 효과, 쉬운 지각적 포착, 흐르는 속도에 대응하는 지연(遲延)의 속성 등이 그러하다. 부전글로컬센터는 건물에서 500m는 뒤로 물러나야 전모가 보이는 스케일이다. 다행히 중앙대로가 8차선의 큰 길이고, 주변이 대형 아파트 단지로 스케일의 맥락을 민감하게 느낄 환경은 아니다. 대신 앞길에서 흐르는 고속도 때문에 작은 스케일은 형태감을 얻기 힘들다.

뒤에 온천천이 있는데, 지각적으로 직결시키기는 어렵지만, 전모를 포착하기에 도시 쪽 보다는 흐드러진 개천 쪽에서 보는 장면이 좋다. 이미 작가도 그 거대 서사로서 표현이 좋았던 모양이다. 자꾸 그 장면을 그린다.

들린 건축

들린 건축, '드는 일'의 은유는 '받는 일'의 사실이다. 이은석 교수의 작품 중에서 부전글로컬센터를 비롯하여 들린 모습의 건축을 항상(恒常)처럼 본다. 푸른 마을교회(경북 포항시, 2004), 상암교회(서울 마포구 상암지구, 2006), 오산교회(부산 해운대구, 2014), 하늘보석교회(충남 서산시, 2014) 그리고 손양원 목사 기념관(경남 함안군, 2015) 등이 그러하다.

몸을 드는 것은 품는 일을 하기 위해 먼저 하는 일이다. 마치 암탉이 날개를 쳐들고 병아리들을 품는 형세이다. 그러니까 '들린 모습'은 '열린 교회'가 되기 위한 첫 번째 몸짓이다. 교회는 거기에서 도시의 일을, 땅의 일을, 사람의 일을, 심성의 일을 끌어들인다. 사람들이 오는 일이고, 교회에 가는 일이다.

1 — 부전글로컬비전센터 이음홀
    Ieum Hall, Bujeon Glocal Vision Center
2 — 푸른 마을교회, 들린 볼륨
    lifted volumes, Green Village Church
3 — 오산교회, 예배실 스테인드글라스
    stained glass of chapel, Osan Curch
4 — 오산교회 전경
    front view, Osan Curch

3

4

반면에 우리는 보통적으로 교회가 무겁게 닫힌, 열기 힘든, 교회가 방어적이라는 아이러니를 자주 본다.

지각심리학으로 보아 '든다'는 것은 인력에 저항하는 쾌감이 있다. 비행이나 바다 위에 떠가는 배처럼 무중력의 욕망이 있는 모양이다. 이은석의 건축은 공중부양을 하려고 한다.

뜨는 공간은 방주이다

그러고 보면 한눈에 그의 알레고리를 방주로 알아보겠다. 큰 방주는 몸을 들고 열어서 안으로 끌어들인 것들을 충분히 담아 갈 만큼 넉넉해 보인다. 선체의 구조는 수개 층에 걸쳐 뭔가를 담는다. 이 방주는 떠나려는 것이 아니라, 긴 항해를 마치고 방금 여기에 정박한 것 같다. 전면에 깊이 꽂힌 닻의 모양 때문이다. 방주는 이제 모든 것을 내려놓을 것이다. 싣고 온 것은 생명이기도 하고 희망이기도 하다.

전면에 솟은 피어는 등대 같기도 하다. 등대의 서사적 뜻은 종교건축에서 익숙하다. 모든 게 막연했던 항해의 끝에서 2016년 12월 25일 새로운 일을 시작했다.

작은 순례

어떤 건축에서 시간을 지체하고 싶다든지, 자꾸 걷게 만드는 것은 이유가 있다. 물론 건축가가 획책한 것이지만, 우리는 그 경험을 '공간 산책'이라고 한다.

그것이 종교건축일 경우, 공간을 공감각하면서, 종교적 수사를 얹었다면 작은 순례길이라 할 만하다. 그러지 않아도 우리는 건축에서 공공 공간을 보다 풍부히 하기를 바란다. 공공

공간에 인색한 건축은 나쁜 건물이다. 기능 또는 수익을 먼저 보는 눈에는 이 공공의 가치가 보이지 않는다. 이은석 교수의 건축이 착한 건축이라는 것은 우선 이 공적 영역을 위해 애쓰는 노력 때문이다.

오산교회에서는 마당과 내부의 공적 공간과 긴 램프와 회유하는 경로가 길다. 손양원 목사 기념관은 그야말로 이야기가 절절한 시간 여행이다.

부전글로컬센터는 들어 올려준 품 안에 중정을 내포하고 있기에 원융(圓融)이 형성된다. 여러 번 회유하는 공간은 자꾸 안팎을 들락날락하기 마련인데 그것이 모두 관계항(關係項)이다. 관계가 많은 건물은 일단 풍족한 공공 공간의 증거이다. 긴 램프로 주변과 내부공간을 경과하니 곧 순례이며, 옥상은 필그림의 종착이다. 옥상공간은 좀 막연한 기분이 있으나, 도시에서는 하늘만으로도 극적이다. 만약 좀 더 종국적 연출을 부추긴다면 종교적 알레고리는 궁극을 만들 것 같다.

영원한 교회의 상징, 빛의 문제

부전글로컬센터의 본당 회중석은 자연광이 차폐된 인조광으로 밝기를 만드는데, 건축가에게는 그것이 안심할 수단이라고 했다. 확실히 천장 전면의 인조광은 균질한 조도로 실내를 밝힌다. 다만 빛이 갖는 풍부한 수사적 성능을 환기한다면, 빛이 표현적이냐 또는 편안한 환경일 것이냐에서 선택은 쉽다. 자연의 빛이 왜 중요한지는 에너지 절약의 문제만이 아니라, 부드러운 공기를 만들기 때문이다.

이은석 교수의 빛은 그가 원칙적으로 강조하면서도 (『아름다운 교회 건축』, 두란노, 2008) 실제에서는 그러하기도

Preface.

종교를 위한 건축적 알레고리
Architectural Allegory for Religion

024

박길룡
국민대학교 건축대학 명예교수
Park, Kil-young.
Emeritus Professor, School of Architecture
Kookmin University

하고 아니기도 하다. 오산교회(부산, 2014)에서 르 꼬르뷔지에는 여전히 유효하며, 빛이 인색하다. 교당의 한쪽 벽에 펀칭된 스테인드글라스는 실내를 거친 간접광이다. 반면에 사월교회(대구, 2009)에서는 후광 채광, 삼각 천창, 기울어진 또는 굴곡진 측창 등으로 풍부하다.

'아름답게 지으니 좋으시더라'

이 글의 화두로 삼은 보편적 공공의 가치로 돌아가 본다. 현대사회에서 교회당의 합목적성은 특수한 것이 아니다. 그것이 사회적 보편성을 갖기 때문에 우리 도시는 이 시설을 근린계획에 두고 있다. 그래서 교회는 담임의 자산도 아니고, 신자들의 내향적 문화로는 곤란하다. 이러한 가치관은 경영의 문제이겠지만, 지금 여기에서는 보편적 공공성을 건축에게 묻는 것이다. 건축이 종교의 이타성으로서, 지역사회가 교회를 공공의 가치로 주고받을 문제이다.

"부전교회는 대개의 교회 건축물이 수직의 첨탑으로 표상되는 관습적인 설계에서 벗어나 있다. 이제 막 돛을 달고 미지의 세상으로 떠나려는 배처럼 자유롭고 호기심 가득한 표정으로 시민들을 기다린다. 딱딱하게 굳어 위압적인 수직성이 아니라, 많은 것을 포용할 듯한 자세로 수평적으로 계속 확산하고 있다." - 부산일보 박태성 문화전문기자

교회당은 그의 상징성 때문에 더 깊은 문화적 격조를 필연으로 한다. 건축은 결국 물상과 공간으로 만들어지는데 부전글로컬센터에서는 이를 '열린 형식'과 '다의적 알레고리'로 말하였다. 교회당은 예배시간에만 작동하는 것이 아니라, 그 존재 자체가 지역사회의 자존심이다. 그것은 내재(空)의 문제와 동시에 외연(色)의 일로서 건축이다.

후기 구조주의 시대에 들어, 우리나라의 교회 건축은 명·암의 양태를 보인다. 우선 양이 급증하면서 양산된 허접스런 건축이 어둡다. 거기에는 종교적 프로퍼갠더, 즉 과시적이고 정치적인 교회의 모습을 포함한다. 밝은 면은 현대건축 상황에서 종교적 보편성이 유독 빛나는 곳이 우리나라라는 사실이다. 우리는 서구에서 기독교를 배웠지만, 구미의 신앙이 헛헛해지고 있는 상황에서, 한국의 기독교 건축은 더 빛나는 생과(生果)로 보인다.

이 이은석의 아윤(雅潤)한 건축, '아름답게 지으니 좋으시더라.'

Architectural Allegory for Religion

Park, Kil-young. Emeritus Professor, School of Architecture Kookmin University

An Architectural Allegory for Religion: Leading the Way to Bujeon Presbyterian Church

After disembarking at Busan station, I got into a taxi and told the driver that I want to get to Bujeon Presbyterian Church, but unfortunately I was not sure at how to best explain the directions. My concern was unfounded, as the driver began to tell me about the story behind the church. He recounted how the church site used to belong to a factory in Songwol Towel, that the landowner had sold the land to the church at a very affordable price, and that construction was made possible because the construction company had offered a huge discount & it was truly remarkable story.

In other words, for someone living in Busan, the Bujeon Presbyterian Church (and perhaps the taxi driver was a member of the church) is a place that is generally and commonly known. Considering that Busan is a metropolitan city, the church is of course different from a small village church, but the Bujeon Presbyterian Church is not on the scale of a world heritage site either. Perhaps the church is well-known for its monumentality and its positioning in the area, which is easy to spot visually, or perhaps the church is best known for its long service to the people of Busan. Regardless, what is significant here is that this church has very much assimilated itself into local society despite its relative youth. My understanding of the church was greatly enhanced thanks to the crash course offered by the taxi driver.

Contemporary Age — Urban City — Church — Hall

I am a free thinker, but I have encountered numerous churches throughout my studies of the history of world architecture. As an important element in the international cultural landscape, I recognise the central position held by religious architecture throughout history, regardless of whether it is in the eastern or western hemisphere.

I take off my hat when I enter the church, and groom myself when I enter a temple (I emphasise again that I am a non-believer). Every location contains a soul, and if it is the place where a god resides I believe that it is a place that transcends our daily lives. However, not all churches seem to possess that soul within their walls. There are many churches where the presence of god has disappeared along with the secularization of religion. Instead, churches that have been influenced by capital and power have become increasingly visible. However, as spaces of grace and spirituality continue to remain pivotal within our society, I believe that a sense of tradition can still be maintained. Then how should we embark on the task of getting to know the soul of a location, and especially in a church?

Generally, this can be understood through religious allegory. Therefore, I arrived at a bold conclusion that an architect is the messenger of that faith. The revival of the arts, after the severity of the gothic style softened with the onset of the renaissance, with humanist principles at its core, prompted the self-contradiction of the Catholic faith in the late renaissance age with extremized papal authority, the encouragement of globalization, the mission of Christianity, the bloody religious reformation and Protestantism. I

1 — 단순한 볼륨, 늘샘교회
      simple volume, Neolsem Church
2 — 범어교회, 100주년 기념교회
      Pomo Church, the 100th anniversary memorial church

1   2

think that Christianity is special, and this is especially true in Korea due to the crucial role it has played in the modernization of the Korean society. The legacy of these historical shifts are present in the history of architecture.

Church buildings were built upon the sites of martyrs who gave their lives to the mission in Chosun, who strove to enlighten the masses while facing cultural opposition, who taught its people of individuality and love, which were human qualities hidden beneath feudalist reign. The church was a significant event for the people of Chosun society, and I remember that it was a doorway to western culture. It supported the independence movement. It was also where people first came to learn about constructing buildings with bricks, about how to build buildings with high peaks, and also to learn of creating a gathering space for a congregation. It helped the people to conceive of a community, and aided significantly in leading them forward in their view towards women and children, love, enlightenment, and democracy.

In this age, Korean Christianity has expanded rapidly (due to its socio-historical significance), many religious studies have been set up in universities, and many pastors are being trained. This led church architecture to merely become one of 'those many things'. In the name of popularizing religion, this attitude is undermining architectural culture. Now, Korean contemporary church architecture divides itself between architectural ignorance (much more authoritative) and a purified consciousness (still a minority, but nevertheless influential). The antisocial aspect, composed of pride and prejudice towards form, excessiveness of symbols, and a obsession with size belong to the world of ignorance. On the other hand, humility towards form, simplistic attitude towards symbol, and a friendly community composes a purified architecture. It seems that the perspective of an onlooker towards church architecture, rather than a religious person, is now necessary.

Professor Architect

The architect Lee Eunseok is also a university professor. A professor architect tends to differ from a normal architect in that they strive continuously to understand architecture methodically and logically. The books of Prof. Lee Eunseok prove that he is an intelligent architect. The title of his book Towards a New Church Architecture may sound a little haughty, but he criticizes directly (with much frustration) the architectural culture of Korea. The expression 'beautiful' in his book Beautiful Church Architecture is not in reference to beauty itself, but to the aesthetics of honesty. Hence, he possesses an investigative and fighting spirit. While he can seem uncooperative at times, he knows how to concede his position when there is a legitimate reason.

It is not that a professor architect or an architecture professor is in an easier position in terms of conducting their architectural practice. Sometimes he finds himself in a situation where his logic restricts him of his freedom, or when a principle prohibits his autonomy. It is a reality that matches, in terms of its difficulty, with the issue of knowing what one should do and should not do. Hence, his 'beauty'

박길룡
국민대학교 건축대학 명예교수
Park, Kil-young.
Emeritus Professor, School of Architecture
Kookmin University

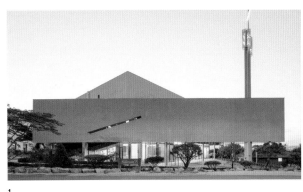

1

2

contains a repressed passion. It restricts oneself from being too liberal, but it also serves as the measuring line of self-control.

The Mega Church and its Spatial Programme

How wide an area does one need in order to appreciate the width of the heavens? To the world, the paradigm of a mega church is something to ponder. From a higher perspective, the church building reflects the church and what it stands for, and therefore when one wishes to stand for many things on the largest possible scale, the church takes on the form of a mega church. The need for church expansions in the contemporary age is one that is understandable and was long anticipated, but one should also adopt a discerning eye as these expansions are sometimes led by greed. I am also well aware of practices such as hereditary succession, management complications, a CEO-style ministry, and so on.

More recently, we note a trend within church programming to expand community activities in earnest. It looks like a cultural structure formed by a new generation of believers in the contemporary age, but there is also the view of environment determinists that states that culture is shaped by its environment. Its grander size would allow such a church to do more great things. However, mega churches are often frowned upon due to a sense of contradiction arising from their monumental size and associated un-religious practices.

The pure size of the space is accounted for by the perceived distance — that is, the size determined by sight,

hearing, a sense of its spatiality, and so on. As the modern church expands in size, it looks unnecessarily troublesome to make artificial adjustments such as installing audio and visual extensions or projections. If the hall capacity is 3,000, it is already large even for a concert hall. The Sejong Cultural Center reduced its number of seats from 4,500 to 3,000, and the Seoul Arts Center can hold 2,500. No matter how large one wants to build a concert hall, there is a limit to its size in terms of acoustics. It is said that the optimum number for conveying musical performances without using loudspeakers is 1,500 seats.

This applies equally to a church. In a huge space, it becomes difficult to focus on the scripture and the message. To make up for this, the service becomes a show or an event. A second congregation floor is installed when the church expands, and this actually creates a bigger problem. Instead of functioning as a space for participating in the service, the second floor becomes a space for watching the service.

The hall in Bujeon Presbyterian Church has a capacity of 3,000, and it takes on a semi-circle arena spatial form. The fan-shaped plane is centripetal, and it is useful in helping one to focus on the service. It also features a behavioural aspect to the structural design, in which everyone can participate in the service on the same floor.

Architectural Allegory

From the belief that architecture can speak and convey meanings, architects found symbols: rhetorical pronouncements shaped into expressions. An extreme example of

this would be the gothic cathedral. However, at the onset of the Renaissance, this more symbolic approach to form was abandoned. As the Baroque age began to expand an understanding of rhetoric, the trend for building architecture in a more extreme way became fashionable. Modernism may have left all preconceptions of meaning and symbolism behind, but it seems that architectural rhetoric begins to recover its relevance in late Modernism. However, this understanding of symbolism and rhetoric has now been made abstract and functions only metaphorically.

There seems to be a certain number of steps requiring attention in order to speak in terms of a symbol, metaphor or allegory, as when discussing literacy in architecture. In the Medieval Gothic period, the entire structure of the church was a symbol. The body (body of Christ), the light (heart of Christ), and the cross (Christ Himself) symbolized religious faith. Furthermore, this holistic impression also extended to the holy artifacts, artworks, and the icons. While not as explicitly visible as symbols, metaphors are intuitively perceived. As literature cannot limit itself to direct facts, metaphors are the life of language, and it is the same for architecture. Allegories are somewhat more flexible. There is room for people to think differently, and it allows for the wider literal expression of the artist.

There is something that I wish to say about Lee Eunseok's architecture, whether referring to architectural symbols or to a specific rhetorical line: his language is often abstract and metaphoric, and so we need to read them closely. I have read the following:

The Model of Size

Sometimes, the size itself can be an aesthetic. There is also beauty or artistic pleasure in something small or large. For something huge, it gives off a spectacular visual effect, it is easy to spot, and it has a property that resists the flowing pace around it. Bujeon Presbyterian Church is on a scale that can only be wholly captured by the eye by stepping back about 500m back from the building.

Fortunately, as the main road is a huge 8-lane road, and because the surroundings are covered with apartment complexes, the scale factor does not come off as significantly important. However, due to the high-speed traffic in the front road, a smaller scale would have made it difficult for Bujeon Presbyterian Church to gain a full sense of form.

Oncheoncheon is also at the back, and while it might be difficult to connect directly in terms of perception, when trying to capture the full-length view, it is better to look towards the sea by the city from the side of the brook. Perhaps the artist too liked the idea of expression as an epic prologue. I keep drawing that image in my mind.

Raised Architecture

Raised Architecture. The metaphor of 'to raise' is based in the fact of 'receiving'.

I keep seeing this kind of 'carried architecture' throughout the work of Prof. Lee Eunseok, particularly in examples such as Bujeon Presbyterian Church. This applies to the Pureun Maeul Church, the Sangam Church, the Osan Church, the Hanuel Boseok Church, the Reverend Son Yang-

종교를 위한 건축적 알레고리
Architectural Allegory for Religion

박길룡
국민대학교 건축대학 명예교수
Park, Kil-young.
Emeritus Professor, School of Architecture
Kookmin University

1   2

won Martyr Memorial Hall, among others.

Raising one's body is an action that one must perform in order to embrace something. It resembles the intention exhibited by the hen that lifts its wings to embrace its chicks. Therefore, the 'raised appearance' is the first step to becoming an 'open church'. From there, the church draws in the labour of the city, the labour of the earth, the labour of man, and the labour of the heart. It is the work of encouraging people to come to church, of inviting people into church. On the other hand, we often observe an ironic situation in which the church is heavily enclosed, hard to open, and seemingly defensive.

When looking from perceptive psychology, 'to raise' indicates a sense of fulfillment that comes from resisting gravity. There seems to be a present desire to be in a state of zero gravity, like a plane in the air or a boat on the water. Lee Eunseok's architecture tries to elevate itself and almost levitate in space.

Floating Space is an Ark

I would like to read his work as an allegory for an ark. A large ark looks roomy enough to carry everything that it has invited inside. The structure of the boat carries many things across its multiple floors. This ark is not about to leave, but looks as if it has anchored recently after a long sail. This is because of the anchor-shaped structure at the front. The ark will now give up everything: it not only brought life, but also hope. The pier that stands erect at the front looks like a lighthouse. The rhetorical meaning of a lighthouse is common in religious architecture. After a long and endless sail, it started a new phase in its life from 25 December 2016.

A Small Pilgrimage

There is a reason why one wishes to spend one's time frequenting and walking around a certain place. Undoubtedly, this was the plan of the architect, but we name that experience the 'spatial stroll'.

If this was a case in religious architecture, the experience of empathising with the space and even with the religious and rhetorical overtones could also perhaps be known as a mini pilgrimage. Even if it's not, we would like to ask for more public space in architecture. An architecture that is not generous in terms of public space is a bad building. The value of a public space is not visible to an eye that merely looks for function or net worth above anything else. It is because of his efforts in the public sector that I consider Prof. Lee Eunseok's works to be good architecture.

Within Osan Church, the public space in the yard and the building, and the route that extends around the long lamp, are long. The Reverend Son Yangwon Martyr Memorial Hall offers an experience of time-travel as it is full of stories. In Bujeon Presbyterian Church, because the central court is contained within an elevated space, a zone of indifference has been created. The space travels back and forth multiple times and tends to move in and out often, and these are all decisive relationships. A building that has many relationships signals a structure of abundant public spaces. By traversing the surroundings and the inner spaces along the

1 ⎯ 세 가지 사랑의 유산을 건축으로 형상화,
    애국지사 손양원 기념관
    embodies three legacies of love in architecture,
    Son Yang-Won Memorial Museum

2 ⎯ 기념관의 역사성과 공간의 공감각,
    애국지사 손양원 기념관
    history of memorial hall and consensus of space,
    Son Yang-Won Memorial Museum

3 ⎯ 빛이 주는 풍부한 수사적 성능, 성광교회
    the facade becomes a luminous body of
    colorful changing light, Holy Light Church

4 ⎯ 환대와 종교성의 다의적 알레고리, 성광교회
    a polysemous allegory of hospitality and religiosity,
    Holy Light Church

3   4

long lamps one is on the pilgrimage, and the rooftop is the destination of the pilgrim. The rooftop space is somewhat vague, but in a city access to the sky itself is already extreme. If something more final and dramatic were to be enacted, I think that the religious allegory would be expressed in its fullest possible sense.

The Eternal Symbol of the Church, and the Problem of Light
The main hall of the Bujeon Presbyterian Church is cut off from natural light, and the congregation seats are brightened by artificial light. It was made clear to the architect that there would be no problem with this solution.
The artificial light on the ceiling plane effectively lightens the room on a homogeneous level. However, when considering the rich rhetorical function of light, it is easy to choose between expressive light and comfortable light. Natural light is important not only because of energy conservation issues, but also because it creates a gentler atmosphere.

Although emphasized in terms of design principles, Prof. Lee Eunseok's ideas concerning light (Beautiful Church Architecture) are sometimes practiced but not always followed to the same degree in reality. Le Corbusier in the Osan Church is still valid and has been preserved against the light. The stained glass placed on one side of the church hall is an indirect light that makes its way across the interior. On the other hand, in the Sawol Church, the lighting is plentiful with aureole lighting, a triangular ceiling, slanted or curved side windows, among other elements.

'He had made it, and it was very good'
I now return to the universal worth of publicity, which I determined as the main topic of this text. The purposefulness of a church building in the contemporary age is not something special. Because it embraces social universality, the city maintains this facility as part of its neighbourhood planning. Hence, the church is not the private property of its leader, nor can it be reduced to an exclusive culture of believers. Such a perspective would constitute a management issue, but what I wish to ask here is a question about universal publicity of architecture. It is about the issue of how architecture can act as the alterity of religion, and how local society can appreciate the church as a public value.

'Bujeon Presbyterian Church does not resemble most church structures, which typically follow the traditional design of a vertical spire tower. Like a boat that is about to pull its anchor and float away to the world of unknowns, it is waiting for its passengers with a free and curious expression. Instead of a hardened and intimidating verticality, it continuously expands itself horizontally with an all-inviting attitude.'
Park Taesung, Culture Correspondent at Busan Ilbo

Because of its symbolic nature, a deeper cultural undertone is necessary for a church building. Architecture is ultimately created through physical things and space, and the Bujeon Presbyterian Church expresses them with an 'open form' and 'polysemantic allegory'. The church does not only exist

Preface.

박길룡
국민대학교 건축대학 명예교수
Park, Kil-young.
Emeritus Professor, School of Architecture
Kookmin University

during the hours of its services— its existence itself is the pride of the region. It is architecture that demonstrates the simultaneous problems of inner space and the work of external colour. As we step into the late age of structuralism, church architecture in Korea tends to adopt a light-dark mode. First of all, due to its explosive increase in number, mass-produced slipshod architecture is dark. Furthermore, this has included the problem of religious propaganda — that is, the conspicuity and the political nature of certain churches. On the bright side, in terms of the situation in contemporary architecture, the fact remains that religious universality is rather well-practiced in Korea. Although we learnt of Christianity from the West, Christian architecture in Korea is beginning to bear bright fruits while the influence of the faith in western regions is beginning to dwindle. The sublime architecture of Lee Eunseok: 'He had made it, and it was good'.

비전,
함께 짓는
아름다운 사역

박성규
부전교회
담임목사

부전교회는 100년을 준비하는 역사와 전통이 살아있는 교회로 잘 알려져 있습니다. 그리고 그 사역이 시작된 장소는 세대를 넘어 중요한 기억을 간직한 곳이 분명합니다. 그런데도 자리를 옮겨 새로운 터에 교회를 짓게 된 배경을 듣고 싶습니다.

두 가지 이유를 들 수 있겠어요. 우선은 1,700여 명이던 교인 수가 2,400명을 넘어가니까 공간의 한계가 왔어요. 이전 교회는 예배실 규모도 작았지만, 지역의 한계도 있었어요. 전통시장에 인접하다 보니 도로가 좁고, 주차도 불편했어요. 차를 타고 왔다가 그냥 돌아가는 사람도 생겼고요. 이런 일들이 장기화되면 교회가 곧 정체되겠다고 판단했어요. 두 번째로는 부산의 신자율이었어요. 2007년 BFGF 프랭클린 그레함 목사 초청 전도집회를 준비하면서 부산의 기독교인이 33만 명이라는 사실을 알았어요. 부산에는 신도 수가 30만 명이 넘는 사찰도 있는데 부산 전체 교인 수가 사찰 하나만도 못하다는 걸 실감했어요. 열심히 전도해서 교회가 더 성장하는 것이 사람을 구원하고 도시를 변화시키는 일이라고 생각했어요. 그래서 건축을 준비하기 시작했고요.

교회를 옮기기로 결정하기까지 쉽지 않았을 것 같습니다.

건축을 준비하면서 교회 역사를 살펴봤어요. 1932년 3월 5일 15명이 아홉 평에서 시작해서 해방 후에 노동훈련소로 쓰던 큰 건물로 이사 갔어요. 6.25전쟁 때 미군이 후퇴하면서 건물을 못 쓰게 되면서 지난번 교회 터로 옮기게 되었어요. 부전교회는 시대적 부름에 따라 하나님의 인도로 과감하게 움직였던 교회였어요. 그래서 성도들을 격려할 수 있었어요. 그런데 비전을 선포한 후에 경제가 점점 어려워지고 있다는 사회적 분위기가 만들어졌어요. 위축되기 쉬운 상황이었죠. 그때 다시 교회사를 봤어요. 우리 교회는 6.25전쟁 중에 천막 예배당에서 모이다가 1951년 예배당을 지었어요. 어려운 시기에 건축했던 거죠. 왜냐하면 교회가 성장하니까요. 두 번째 예배당은 석유파동이 닥쳤던 1973년, 교육관은 IMF 때 지었어요. 그래서 경제 위기를 이유로 성장의 움직임을 멈춰서는 안된다고 독려할 수 있었어요. 교회의 오랜 역사가 걸림돌이 되기보다는 새로운 동기부여가 된 것이죠. 부전교회는 어려운 시기마다 성장하고 필요할 때마다 움직이는 교회, 유목민적 과감성을 가진 교회

라고 성도들이 공감하게 되었어요.

건축을 결정하기 전에 고쳐 쓰기로 계획하고 리모델링도 했다고 들었습니다. 집을 고치고 이사하기로 결정하기까지 정말 다른 의견들이 많았을 것 같습니다.

그렇죠, '큰돈 들여서 고치고 꼭 이사해야 하나'라고 반문할 수 있죠. 그런데 교우들이 비전을 공감해서 잘 따라와 줬어요. 그리고 이 처소를 상업적인 시설에 팔지 않고, 이단이 아닌 건강한 교회가 쓸 수 있게 된다면 아깝지 않다고 생각했어요. 그래서 정말 다른 교회에 낮은 금액으로 넘겨주고 나오게 되었습니다.

처음에 이 교회 터를 보시고 여기에 어떤 교회를 지어야겠다고 생각했나요?

평소 제가 고민했던 교회론을 생각했어요. 세상과 분리되지 않은 교회, 세상 속의 교회, 세상에 영향을 주는 교회, 세상 사람들이 들어올 수 있는 교회였지요. 이런 교회를 만들기 위해서는 개방성이 가장 중요했어요. 그리고 선교에 대한 비전을 생각했어요. 교회에는 수평적인 세계선교와 다음 세대를 위한 수직적인 선교가 모두 필요하거든요. 영국의 교회가 실패한 원인은 수평적인 선교는 했지만, 어린이와 청소년, 청년들에게 복음을 전하는 수직 선교를 간과했어요. 모 교회가 흔들리면 선교도 끝나게 되죠. 그래서 우리는 다음 세대에 중점을 두면서 동시에 지역사회의 복음화에 끊임없이 노력해야겠다고 생각했어요. 지역 주민들이 함께하지 않으면 세계 선교도 힘을 잃게 되니까요. 그래서 만든 단어가 글로컬(global + local)입니다.

그런 생각을 가지고 코마건축의 안을 결정하게 된 것인가요?

코마건축의 계획안을 보고 무릎을 '탁' 쳤어요. 그렇지만 공정한 심사를 위해서 저는 의견을 말하지 않았어요. 심사위원들이 엄정한 절차를 거쳐 진행했기 때문에 공통의 의견이 모이길 기다렸죠. 우선 코마건축의 안이 마음에 들었던 것은 개방성이었어요. 시민 누구나 들어올 수 있도록 열려 있었어요. 그리고 교회 건물은 대개 비슷하다는 생각을 떨쳐버릴 만큼 독특

박성규
부전교회 담임목사
Park Sung-kyu.
Pastor,
Bujeon Presbyterian Church

했어요. 교회가 지어질 위치가 섬과 같아서 어디서나 잘 보이고, 멀리서도 눈에 띄는 곳이에요. 그래서 그냥 지나칠 수 없을 만큼 즐거움과 관심을 끄는 형상이 좋았습니다. 물론 땅의 모양을 최대한 활용하여 짜임새 있게 쓴 점도 마음에 들었습니다.

보통 몇몇 교회의 예처럼 건물이 커지면 화려한 이미지는 배로 늘어납니다. 호텔은 화려하길 바라지만 교회는 검소하길 바라는 사람들의 시선도 부담스러워지고요. 마침 노출 콘크리트 외관이 원하는 인상을 줄 수 있을 것 같았어요. 물론 자칫 도시의 거대한 흉물이 될 수도 있다는 걱정도 있었고요.

저도 건물을 많이 보러 다녔는데 노출 콘크리트가 이렇게 시공된 건물은 처음입니다. 이런 규모의 면적을 한 번에 맞추기는 정말 어려운 일입니다. 깜짝 놀랐습니다.

경동건설의 노력이 컸던 것 같아요. 정말 귀한 분을 만났습니다. 덕분에 처음에 상상했던 그 이상의 모습으로 구현된 것 같습니다. 경동건설 회장님이 마음껏 지원해주셨기에 가능했다고 봅니다.

이제 교회 안에 다양한 공간이 만들어졌습니다. 계획과 함께 구상했던 지역사회를 향한 다양한 활동이 시작되는 건가요?

일단 웨딩 채플이 공간 기부의 좋은 모델이 될 텐데요. 사회 저소득층이나 다문화 가족처럼 경제적으로 어려운 분들에게는 무료 대여할 계획입니다. 물론 어느 정도 경제적 여유가 있는 분들에게는 실경비와 운영비를 받아야겠죠. 수익을 가지고 어려운 이웃을 돕는 쪽으로 환원하는 거죠. 그리고 공연장에서는 뮤지컬이나 음악 공연을 열고, 체육관이나 어린이 극장은 주변 학교와 어린이집, 유치원에서 사용할 수 있도록 최대한 배려할 계획입니다.

외부공간은 특별한 계획이 있나요? 천변에서 걸어오다 보면 들어가 보고 싶다는 생각이 듭니다. 산책하던 분들이 교회를 많이 찾아올 것 같습니다.

장기적인 계획은 옥상에 하늘정원을 만들어서 시민들이 자연스럽게 올라가서 차를 마시며 머물 수 있는 장소로 만드는 거죠. 건물에 관한 관심도 높아서 해설사와 함께하는 건물 투어 프로그램도 필요할 것 같아요.

교회를 건축하면서 가장 어려웠던 점과 보람을 느꼈을 때는 언제였나요? 결정적 순간 같은 것이 있었을 것 같은데요.

비가 많이 와서 홍수가 난 적이 있어요. 온천천이 비가 오면 금방 불어나거든요. 5천 톤의 물이 이쪽으로 들어왔어요. 문제가 될까 긴장했었어요. 그리고 공사 시작 전에는 암반이 없다고 파악했는데 지하 4층 면에서 연암반이 나와서 다이너마이트를 사용할 수밖에 없었죠. 지하철하고 9m 거리인 곳도 있어서 혹시라도 선로에 이상을 줄까 조마조마한 적도 있고요. 다행히 잘 끝나서 참 감사했습니다.

지금 교인들은 어떤 장소를 제일 좋아하나요?

교회학교가 접하고 있는 선큰 가든이 제일 반응이 좋고요. 아이들이 자유롭게 뛰어놀 수 있는 곳이라 늘 활력이 넘치는 곳이죠. 그리고 캔틸레버 밑 광장도 청년들에게 인기가 좋아요. 입구에 마련된 어린이 도서관도 책이 들어가기 시작해서 이제 북적거리고 있고요. 주중에는 주변 어린이집이나 유치원에서도 많이 찾아올 것 같아요.

이제 새로운 예배당을 짓고 새로운 동력으로 교회를 움직여야 하는데, 과거와 달라진 점이 있다면 무엇일까요?

이렇게 예배당을 크게 짓고자 한 가장 큰 목적은 많은 시민의 구원이고요. 두 번째는 점점 탈기독교화되는 다음 세대를 붙잡기 위한 것이에요. 그 사람들이 예수님을 마음껏 만날 수 있는 장소가 되는 것이 이곳의 가장 큰 존재 이유입니다. 그리고 교회가 어느 정도 자리를 잡으면 독립된 개척 교회 설립을 지원하고 싶어요. 이런 움직임이 한국 교회에 새로운 활력을 불어넣을 것으로 생각하고 있어요.

80주년 영상에서 '모뉴먼트보다는 무브먼트'라는 인상적인 메시지를 보았습니다. 그런 의지를 갖고 있었기 때문에 이런 건물이 세워졌고, 이 집을 통해서 새로운 사람들이 세워지고 또 다른 꿈을 꿀 수 있겠구나 생각했습니다.

제가 만든 말은 아니고요. 책에서 인용한 말인데, 건물을 지을 때도 중요한 슬로건이 되었죠. 우리가 과거에 얽매이지 말고 미래를 향하여 나아가야 한다는 말씀에 충실하다면 분명히 이곳을 세우신 하나님의 뜻을 따라 무브먼트가 일어날 것 같아요.

마지막으로 지난 몇 년간의 경험을 통해 교회 건축을 꿈꾸는 사람들에게 꼭 해주고 싶은 이야기가 있다면 말씀해주십시오.

하나님은 교회가 어떻게 나아가길 원하실까? 그리고 성도들은 어떻게 생각하고 있을까? 기도하며 돌아봐야 합니다. 예배당을 크게 짓는 것보다 어떤 목회철학으로 어떤 사역을 감당해야 할까 먼저 생각해야 합니다. 모든 교회가 해왔던 옛 습관과 방식보다는 하나님의 부르심과 시대적 소명을 깊이 묵상하면서 예배당 건축을 시작하면 그 길이 보일 것입니다.

시간이 지나서 더 풍성하게 이곳이 살아 움직이는 모습을 보러 다시 한 번 방문하고 싶습니다. 오늘 말씀 감사합니다.

인터뷰_ 김혁준(픽셀하우스 편집장)

1 ─── 닮음아트홀 공연모습
performance of Daum Art Hall
2 ─── 부전교회(부전동) 이전 모습
Bujeon Presbyterian Church (before)

Vision: Constructing Together a Beautiful Ministry

Park Sung-kyu. Pastor, Bujeon Presbyterian Church

Bujeon Church is well-known for its history and tradition that extends for almost a century. The original site of the ministry must hold multitude of memories and significance for many generations. Tell us hear more about the background to the project and why you decided to build a new church on this particular site.

I can think of two reasons. First, the building could not accommodate all of the members of our congregation when the number increased from 1,700 to 2,400. The original building was limited due to its small room for worship but also because of its location. Located next to the traditional market, the church was also blighted by a narrow access way and awkward parking. People were often forced to leave, as they were unable to find a parking space. I thought that this situation would hamper the growth of the church in the long run. The second reason was the number of church goers in Busan. In preparation for the Busan Franklin Graham Festival (BFGF) in 2007, I noted that there were only 330,000 Christians in Busan. A Single Buddhist temple here in Busan had more than 300,000 members, exceeding the total number of Christians in Busan. I thought the growth of a church, as part of an evangelistic mission, had the potential to save people and change our city. Therefore, I began to prepare the construction of a new church building.

However, it must have been a difficult decision to relocate the church.

I reviewed the history of my church while making the relevant preparations for construction. Established on 5 March 1932 by fifteen people on a 30 site, the church moved to a larger building, formerly used as a labour training post after 1945. The building became unavailable during the Korean War after US troops retreated, and it was relocated to the site before this construction. Bujeon Church has made bold moves under the guidance of God and responded to the request of the times. In this way, I was able to encourage the congregation.

After I declared the vision for the site, a social atmosphere began to take hold that highlighted a worsening economy. The situation was discouraging, but then I read the chronicle of the church again. Gathering in a tent chapel during the Korean War, we built a chapel in 1951. The church was constructed in difficult times, because it was growing rapidly. The second chapel was built during the oil shock in 1973, and the educational hall was constructed during the Asian Financial Crisis. Based on these facts, I encouraged the people not to stop growing in number. The extensive history of the church played as a new motivation rather than a hindrance. People gradually agreed that Bujeon Church grew in difficult times, acting whenever necessity occurred and developing a nomadic courage.

I heard that you had planned to renovate the church and have carried out the remodeling before you actually decided to build the new one. There must have been a diverse range of opinions regarding those decisions.

Yes, you can say, 'Do we have to move after spending a fortune on repairs?' But the church members followed my vision. I thought that it would be worth it to hand over the old church to another sound church instead of selling this place to a commercial facility or to heresy. Thus, we really handed over the building to another church at a lower price.

What kind of church did you want to build when you saw the site for the first time?

I have always contemplated the idea of the church. Openness was the most important factor, as I think that a church should be connected to the world, lie in the world, influence the world, and encourage other people into its fold. I thought about a possible vision for this mission. The church must continue both on a horizontal mission towards the world and a vertical mission for the next generation. The churches in England could be thought to have failed as they have carried out a horizontal mission, but as a result have overlooked the importance of a vertical mission to preach the gospel to their children and youth. When the mother church becomes unstable, missions cannot continue. So, we concluded that by focusing on the next generation, we can make continuous attempts to evangelize the community at the same time. If there is no participation from local people, then the world mission will lose momentum. So we chose the term 'glocal' (global + local).

Did you decide on the design proposal of Atelier KOMA from such a standpoint?

I was so much impressed by KOMA's design, but I concealed my opinion to secure an impartial judging process. As the committee obeyed a strict procedure, I waited for them to draw a consensus. First, it was openness of KOMA's proposal that moved me. It was open to everybody and the church building was unique enough to shake off the idea that church buildings usually follow a similar style. The site of the new church is isolated like an island so that it can be seen from everywhere and made visible from afar. I loved its outstanding shape, one that can give pleasure and attract a range of interests. Of course, I also liked the fact that the proposal made full use of the shape of the site.

As we can see in some churches, the bigger a church building becomes, loudly luxurious the image ap-

pears. While hotels may prefer to be glamorous, churches take care of people who expect them to be simple. I thought that the exposed concrete façade could make the impression I wanted. Of course, it was feared that it would become a huge eyesore in Busan.

I have visited a lot of buildings, but I have never seen any building that used exposed concrete in this way. It is very difficult to implement the technique on this large scale all at once. I was greatly surprised.

I think Kyungdong Construction made a great deal of effort. It was a great honor for me to meet such a nice person. I think the church construction was executed much better than expected. I believe that this was possible thanks to the full support from the CEO of Kyungdong Construction.

Now the new church is equipped with various spaces. Are you going to initiate a variety of activities you envisioned for the community with the plan?

The wedding chapel is a good example of facility usage. We are going to rent it free of charge to the financially challenged, such as the lower-income class or multicultural families. Of course, we will charge those who can afford real expenses and operating expenses. We are planning to help poorer neighbors with the profits. We will present musicals and concerts in the theatre, and try to open gymnasiums and children's theatres to schools, daycare centers and kindergartens in the neighborhood as much as possible.

Do you have any special plans for outdoor space? Seen from the riverside, the building looks inviting. Many neighbors are likely to visit the church.

In the long term, we have a plan to build a sky garden on the rooftops so that people can go up there to drink and rest. The building itself is attracting more interest, and so it seems more and more necessary to launch a guided tour program.

When did you feel most challenged and most rewarded during the process of construction? I think you experienced a decisive moment.

At one point, the site flooded due to heavy rain.

비전, 함께 짓는 아름다운 사역
Vision: Constructing Together a Beautiful Ministry

박성규
부전교회 담임목사
Park Sung-kyu.
Pastor,
Bujeon Presbyterian Church

The Oncheon Stream rises quickly when it rains. Five thousand tons of water overflowed into the area. I was nervous, as it could have caused some serious problems. In addition, no rock was detected before the start of construction, but a soft rock bed was found at the level of the fourth basement and so we had to use dynamite. I felt anxious about this, as one part was only nine metres from the subway tunnel. Fortunately, everything went well, and I thanked God so much!

What is the favorite place for the church members?

The sunken garden, adjacent to the church school, is favored by members. The place is always full of vitality as children can play freely there. The plaza under the cantilever is also popular among young adults. The children's library near the entrance is also crowded as it is filling up with books. I think that many children from nearby childcare centers and kindergartens will visit on weekdays.

Now that you have to run this new church with a renewed driving force, what do you think marks it out as different from that of the past?

The main purpose of building such a large chapel is the salvation of many citizens. Second, we targeted the next generations, many of whom are departing the Christian faith. To create a place in which they can meet Jesus is the most important reason for its existence. I would like to support the establishment of independent church plants once when Bujeon Church is more settled. I think this move will bring a new vitality to Korean churches.

In the 80th anniversary movie clip, I remember the impressive message of 'movement rather than monument'. I thought that as you have been motivated by such an inten-tion, you could build this church and dream another dream by supporting the people here.

I didn't coin the phrase. I quoted it from a book, and it was an important slogan for me during construction. We should not be caught up in the past but head for the future. If we are faithful to the Word, I think that the movement will take place according to the will of God who has established this place.

Finally, do you have any advice gathered over the past few years that you would like to share with people who plan to construct a new church?

Which direction does God want churches to follow? And what kind of opinions do the church members have? We must pray and think back over time. What kind of philosophy should we take forward when we fulfill a ministry rather than building a large chapel? We should think this first. We will find the way when you start to build a chapel, meditating deeply on the calling of God and history, rather than on the old habits and ways that every church has followed.

I would like to visit this place again, particularly when it becomes more vibrant in the future. Thank you very much.

Interviewer_ Kim Hyoukjoon (Director, Pixelhouse)

불가능하기에
시작한 도전

김재진
경동건설 회장

부전교회와의 인연은 어떻게 시작되었나요?

　　평소 알고 지내던 부전교회 신도 한 분이 저에게 자문하러 왔어요. 옛 송월타월 공장 부지에 교회를 신축할 계획인데 어떻게 지어야 후회가 없겠냐는 것이었죠. 건물이 들어설 자리도 그렇고 집회 장소라는 특성도 그렇고, 작품성이 있으면 좋겠다 싶더군요. 그래서 부산국제건축문화제에 공모 하거나, 건축가 추천을 받아서 설계하라고 권유했어요. 그러고는 부산건축문화제 사무국장과 부전교회 관계자 사이에 다리를 놔주고 저는 까마득하게 잊고 있었죠.

설계 도면을 받았을 때 첫인상이 어땠나요?

　　총 다섯 개 업체가 입찰에 참여했어요. 그때 도면을 처음 접했는데 깜짝 놀랐죠. 작품에서 강한 메시지가 느껴졌거든요. 건축가가 그만큼 고심했다는 증거이겠지요. 가장 시선을 끈 건 배를 형상화한 외형이었어요. 항구 도시인 부산이 그 안에 있었어요. 건물 하나에 사회 전체를 담는다는 건 굉장히 힘든 일이잖아요. 50년 넘게 부산에서 일하면서 도시의 의미를 담은 건축은 처음 봤어요. 그리고 또 하나, 예술성이 강한 건물은 비율이 안 맞기 쉬운데 시공사 입장에서 봐도 균형감이 있더군요. 그런데 세부 내용을 찬찬히 뜯어볼수록 겁이 났어요. 잘못하면 사고치겠다 싶어서요. 작품은 멋져도 난해한 건물이라는 현실 인식에 부딪힌 거죠. 고민되던 차에 마침 가격 조건이 맞지 않아 옳다구나 하고 포기해 버렸어요.

시공을 맡기로 결심을 굳힌 계기가 있었겠죠? 뒷이야기를 들려주세요.

　　부전교회에서 상당히 적극적이었어요. 목사님이 두 번이나 사무실로 오셔서 경동건설에서 시공하게 해달라고 기도하다 가시고, 장로님들도 결정날 때까지 집에 못 간다 버티시고. 불교 신자인 제가 얼마나 난감했겠어요(웃음). 나는 못 한다, 교회는 해야 한다, 실랑이가 두 달 반은 지속됐어요. 상황이 그러니까 저도 고민이 돼서 도면을 계속 봤는데 보면 볼수록 난해한 거예요. 그런데 그 와중에 '만약 우리가 아닌 남이 한다면 이 건물이 어떻게 될까'라는 데 생각이 미쳤어요. 건방진 소리로 들리겠지만 '대한민국에서 우리만큼 이 건물을 해석하고 소화할 회

사가 있을까, 내가 책임을 회피하는 건 아닌가'라는 물음표가 제 머릿속을 떠나지 않았죠. 게다가 이 건물은 부산이라는 도시를 가꾸는 조형물이 될 텐데, 내가 태어나고 자란 도시에 가치를 불어넣는 일을 해야 한다는 일종의 소명의식도 있었어요. 결국 계약서에 도장을 찍었죠.

시공상 어려움이 계약을 주저하게 한 큰 요인이었겠죠?

　　건물의 표면 둘레가 260m쯤 돼요. 남북을 가로지르는 길이는 최소 80m에 이르고요. 거기에 두께가 20여센티미터에 불과한 판을 공중에 달아내는 거예요. 높이라도 일정하면 무게가 똑같이 실리니까 괜찮은데, 높이는 물론 각도도 다르고 두께까지 얇으니 자칫하면 뒤틀림이 생길 것 같았어요. 그런 부분까지 생각해서 원가 분석을 했지만 어림잡아 10% 손실을 감수해야겠더군요. 그래서 제가 임원진에 양해를 구했어요. 우리에게 10% 내외의 손실이 발생할 거다. 그러나 이런 훌륭한 작품을 배당받기가 쉽지 않다. 내가 이 업에 종사한 지 50년이 넘었고, 사업을 시작한 지 40년 남짓 됐지만, 이런 건물은 앞으로 오지 않을 거다. 우리에게 맡겨진 사회적 책무로 생각하고, 처음이자 마지막이라는 마음으로 경동이 한번 해 보자. 마침 공사를 시작할 때가 창립 40돌이라 40주년 기념사업이라는 의미를 부여하면서 임직원들을 독려했죠.

노출 콘크리트에 대한 부담도 만만치 않았을 것 같아요.

　　예전에 수가화랑을 노출 콘크리트로 지었어요. 당시에는 만족할 만한 성과를 얻지 못했어요. 몇 번의 수정을 통해 콘크리트 면을 완성해야 했어요. 물론 겉보기에 깨끗하니까 건물주나 일반인들은 만족했어요. 그러나 전문인으로서는 양심에 가책을 받았죠. 수가화랑이라는 전적 때문에 부전교회를 맡기가 더 조심스러웠어요. 한국에서 노출 콘크리트 건물로 손꼽힐 건물이니까요. 그러나 세상에 실패 없이 바르게 깨닫는 일이 없다고, 수가화랑의 실패가 부전교회의 성공으로 이어졌어요.

실제로 노출 콘크리트 완성도 때문에 칭찬이 자자해요.

　　설계한 이은석 교수가 세계에서 제일 잘 됐다고 그래요. 노출 콘크리트를 즐겨 쓰는 일본 건축물을 여럿 둘러봤

Interview.

불가능하기에 시작한 도전
A challenges to Mission impossible

044

김재진
경동건설 회장
Kim Jae-jin.
Chairman, Kyungdong Construction Co. Ltd.

고, 안도 다다오가 지은 것도 자세히 살펴봤지만 우리 것처럼 노출 표면 선이 살아있지 않아요. 개인적으로도 앞으로 노출 콘크리트를 이보다 더 잘할 자신이 없어요. 노출 콘크리트는 말 그대로 마감 없이 민낯을 그대로 드러내는 기법이잖아요. 실수가 용납 안 되죠. 그래서 시공 전부터 고심이 많았어요. 부전글로컬비전센터 현장에 나가면 간부들에게 신신당부했어요. '아흔 아홉 번 잘해도 백 번째 실수하면 아무 소용없다. 잘못되면 뜯어고칠 거냐. 설령 수정이 가능하다 해도 결국 표시가 난다. 자만하지 말고 방심하지 말고 혼신의 힘을 다해서 신경 써 달라'고 말이죠. 집은 정성으로 지어지는 거예요. 구두 닦는 것과 이치상 다를 바가 없어요. 관심 없이 집중하지 않는데 어떻게 광이 나겠어요. 좋은 시멘트 재료를 써서 철저한 사전 점검 후에 정성을 다해 발라야 완벽한 결과물을 기대할 수 있겠죠. 교회 벽면에 150개가 넘는 창이 있는데 메운 곳이 하나도 없어요. 제가 직원들에게 그랬어요. 콘크리트 벽이 하늘이라면 창은 별이다. 그러니 포인트를 망쳐서는 안 된다고요. 다행히 직원들이 잘 따라줘서 어디 내놔도 부끄럽지 않을 건물이 완공됐어요.

공사가 성공적으로 끝난 지금 시점에서 느끼는 소회가 있다면?

건축인으로서 예술성과 작품성이 강한 건물을 짓는 데 일조했다는 점, 그것도 대과 없이 마무리했다는 점에서 큰 보람을 느껴요. 경동건설이 아니면 못했을 어려운 일을 했다는 주변의 인사를 많이 받았어요. 아마 현대건설이나 삼성물산이라면 이렇게 짓지 못했을 거예요. 회사 구성원들도 저와 같은 마음이에요. '경동건설이 이런 일을 할 수 있는 회사구나'라는 긍지를 갖게 됐죠. 회사가 정신적으로 한 단계 성장한 듯해요. 어떤 면에서는 부전교회가 시공사 선택을 잘했다고 볼 수 있어요. 건물을 해석하고 소화하는 능력이 따라줘야 가능한 공사였는데 다행히 경동건설이 두 가지 능력을 갖추고 있었으니까요. 그렇지만 다른 면에서는 경동건설 역시 기회를 잘 포착했어요. 제가 교회 관계자들에게 '우리에게 이런 기회를 줘서 고맙다'는 말을

하곤 해요. 이번 공사에서 10%를 웃도는 손실을 보았지만 저희가 얻은 기회에 비하면 아무 것도 아니에요. 좋은 기회를 잘 소화했다는 데 자부심을 느끼고 만족하고 있어요.

경동건설의 비전 혹은 앞으로의 계획을 말씀해주세요.

건축인으로서, 전문인으로서 상식적으로 일하고 싶은 게 제 바람이에요. 저는 17살에 건축과에 입학해서 56년째 같은 지역에서 한 가지 업에 몸담았어요. 지금까지 그래왔듯이 무리하지 않고 사회의 변화를 따라 회사를 경영할 거예요. 앞으로 5년간 더 일할 여건이 된다면 50주년을 채우고 은퇴하고 싶은 마음도 있어요. 32살에 단독주택 두 채 값이던 300만 원으로 경동건설을 창업했는데, 82살이 되면 딱 50년이 돼요. 웬만해선 기업 수명이 50년을 넘기 어렵다고들 하죠. 설령 그만큼 못 채운다 해도 후회는 없어요. 제가 받은 혜택을 건축계를 위해 기여하면서 살아갈 거니까요.

인터뷰_ 김혁준(픽셀하우스 편집장)

A challenges to
Mission impossible

Kim Jae-jin.
Chairman,
Kyungdong Construction
Co. Ltd.

How did your relationship with Bughen church begin?

One of the non-believers who I usually knew came to ask me. I plan to build a new church on the old Song-wol towel factory site. It is also the place where the building is opened and the characteristic of the meeting place. So, I invited you to make a contest for the Busan Architecture International Cultural Festival or to get a recommendation from the artist. Then I set off a bridge between the executive director of the Busan Architecture Festival and the officials of the Dukje church, and I forgot about it.

What was your first impression when you received the design drawing?

A total of five companies participated in the bid. I was surprised when I first saw the drawing. I felt a strong message in my work. This is proof that the writer was so concerned. The thing that attracted the most attention was the appearance that shaped the ship. Busan, a port city, was in it. It is very difficult to have a whole society in one building. I've been working in Busan for over 50 years. And another thing, the buildings with strong artistry are easy to fit in proportion, but there is a sense of balance in terms of the construction company. But I was scared the more I tortured the details. I want to crash in the wrong way. The work was confronted with reality recognition that it is a wonderful and difficult building. I was worried that the price was not right for the car I was worried about, and I gave up.

There was a time when you were determined to take charge

of construction. Please tell me your back story.

I was very active in the defunct church. The pastor came to the office twice and prayed for the construction at Kyungdong E & C, and the elders persisted not to go home until they decided. How much I would have suffered as a Buddhist (laughs). I can not do it, the church has to do it, it's been two and a half months. So, I was worried about the situation, so I continued to look at the drawings. But in the middle of it, I thought, 'What would happen to this building if it were not for us?' It sounds like a cheeky sound, but the question mark, "Is there a company that can interpret and digest this building in Korea as much as we do, and I avoid the responsibility," did not leave my head. In addition, this building will be a sculpture to decorate the city of Busan. There was also a kind of calling ceremony that I had to work to bring value to the city where I was born and grew up. I finally got the seal on the contract.

The difficulty of construction was a major factor that made the contract hesitant, right?

The surface of the building is about 260m. The length across the North and South reaches at least 80m. I'm putting a plate in the air that's only 20 centimeters thick. If the height is constant, the weight is the same, so it is okay, but the height and the angle are different and the thickness is thin, so it will be distorted. I thought of that part of the cost analysis, but I would have to assume a 10% loss. So I asked my board of directors for your understanding. We will have a loss of about 10%. However, it is not easy to get such a splendid work. I have been in this business for more than 50 years and have been in business for over 40 years, but this building will not come forward. Think of it as the social responsibility entrusted to us, and let Kyungdong do it once and for all. It was 40th anniversary when we started construction work.

I guess the burden on exposed concrete was not too much.

Previously, I built a gallery with exposed concrete. At that time, I did not get satisfactory results. I had to complete the concrete surface with a few modifications. Of course, it was seemingly clean, so the builders and the public were satisfied. However, as a professional, he was taken by conscience. I was more careful to take on the defunct church because of the monument of being a gallery. It is a building that is considered as exposed concrete building in Korea. However, the failure of the gallery did not lead to the success of the defunct church.

In fact, the compliment of exposed concrete is complimented.

Professor Lee Eun-seok who designed it is the best in the world. I have looked around many Japanese buildings that enjoy exposed concrete, and I have looked closely at what was built by Ando Tadao, but the exposed surface lines are not alive as we are. Personally, I can not afford to do better than this. Exposed concrete is a technique that literally exposes people without a deadline. A mistake can not be tolerated. So I had a lot of trouble before construction. When I went to the scene of the Bughen church, I was relieved of the executives. Ninety - nine times good, no hundredth mistake is useless. If it goes wrong, you'll fix it. Even if it can be corrected, it will eventually be displayed. Do not be bragging, do not be vigilant, but do it with all your might. The house is built with care. It is no different than shoe polish. How can I get a sense of not focusing without attention. After a thorough preliminary inspection using good cement material, you can expect to get perfect results with care. There are over 150 windows on the wall of the church. I told my employees. If the concrete wall is sky, the window is a star. So do not ruin your points. Fortunately, the staff was very good, so the building was not overshadowed.

If there is a subcommittee that you feel at this point when the construction is completed successfully?

As a builder, I feel a great reward because I helped build a building with a strong artistic and workability, and finished it without any fuss. I received a lot of greetings from the surrounding area saying that it was difficult to do otherwise. Hyundai E & C or Samsung E & C could not have done so. The members of the company are like me. I got the pride that 'Kyungdong E & C is a company that can do such a thing'. The company seems to have grown mentally. In some ways, it can be said that the defunct church was good at choosing a construction company. Fortunately, Kyungdong E & C had the ability to interpret and digest the building. On the other side, however, Kyungdong E & C also seized the opportunity well. I would say to church officials, 'Thank you for giving us this opportunity.' I saw a loss of over 10% in this construction, but nothing compared to the opportunity we got. I'm proud to have a good opportunity to digest and I'm satisfied.

Please tell us your vision or vision for KyungDong E & C.

As a builder, it is a good idea to work as a professional. I entered the Department of Architecture at the age of 17 and moved to the same area for 56 years. As we have done so far, we will manage our company according to the changes of society without overdoing it. If you are going to be able to work for another five years, you have a feeling that you want to retire with the 50th anniversary. At the age of 32, I started Kyongdong Construction with 3 million won in money, which was worth two houses, but now it is only 50 years when I am 82 years old. It is said that the life expectancy of a company is difficult to exceed 50 years. Even if it does not fill that much, there is no regret. I will live with my contribution to the architecture.

Interviewer_ Kim Hyoukjoon(Director, Pixelhouse)

OPEN

PART 1

눈을 들어
마음을 열다

Open one's eyes and
one's mind

지경을 넓히다
준비된 땅으로

BGVC 터는 부산시 동래구 사직동
옛 송월타월 공장이 있던 자리로 잘 알려진 곳이다.
2000년대 초에 송월타월이 경상남도 양산으로
본거지를 옮기면서 남게 된 이 땅은 금정구, 동래구,
연제구를 가로지르는 온천천과 중앙대로, 1호선 지하철의
흐름에 인접해 있다. 회복된 자연의 풍요로움과 도시의
활력이 공존하는 선택받은 땅이다.

Broaden our Horizons Towards a Prepared Land

The site of the BGVC is well known as the former Songwol
towel factory of Sajik-dong, Dongrae-gu, Busan. It has
been left unoccupied since the relocation of Songwol
Towel to Yangsan, Gyeongsangnam-do in the early 2000s,
and the site is adjacent to the Oncheon Stream, which
passes through Geumjeong-gu, Dongraegu, and Yeon-
je-gu, Chungangdae-ro, and the Busan Subway Line One.
It is a privileged location where one can enjoy both the
richness of a natural landscape restored and the vitality
of the city.

1

자연을 무대로 하여 서 있는 건물의 디자인은,
그 자연이 도시이든 농촌이든, 그 건물이 딛고 서 있는 땅,
그리고 그 건물의 배경을 이루는 하늘에
반응하여 만들어져야만 한다.*

제임스 폴쉐크 (1930-)

1 —— 온천천과 지하철 너머로 보이는 시가지 속 BGVC
     BGVC in urban areas, scenery beyond subway railway and Oncheoncheon
2 —— 옥상에서 내려다보는 동래 지하철역사 주변
     scenery around Dongrae subway station

2

James Polshek (1930-)

The design of buildings in natural settings,
whether urban or rural, must be
responsive to the earth out of which they arise
and the sky against which they are seen.

* 『건축가, 건축을 말하다』에서 발췌
『The Architect Says: Quotes, Quips, and Words of Wisdom』

감각을 깨우다
상상하거나, 경험해보지 못한

BGVC는 다양한 스케일의 공간으로
우리의 감각을 자극한다. 일상에선 경험할 수 없는
거대한 지붕 밑 공간, 수백 명의 사람들이
동시에 올라갈 수 있는 넓은 계단과 하늘로 이어진 길,
그 길 가운데 만나는 콘크리트 숲의 열주 공간 등.
이 땅을 살아가는 사람들이 만나고 모이고
나누는 장소로 살아날 공간이다.

Evoking a Feeling beyond Imagination and
One's Experience

Spaces of various scales in the BGVC stimulate our sens-
es. A huge vaulted space under a roof is very rarely found
in everyday life, a wide staircase which can accommodate hundreds of people at the same time, a road leading
to the sky, and a corridor like a concrete forest in the
middle of the road: these are all elements that cultivate a
place for people to meet, gather and share.

1 —— 웅장한 캔틸레버가 조성하는 추상적 구조미
the beauty of the structure that magnificent cantilever makes

2 —— 하늘을 향해 열린 문
a door opened to the sky

1

최고의 충족감은 건물이 마침내 문을 열고   모세 사프디(1938-)
사람들이 그 건물을 차지할 때 온다.
탯줄을 잘라줬더니 금세 새로운 삶을 살아가는 거다.
이보다 더 큰 만족은 없다.*

1 ─── 적층된 입면에서 표현되는 다양한 내부 기능
        various internal functions that exposed on the surface

2 ─── 거대하게 들린 볼륨으로 도시 속 방주를 형상화
        imagery of an urban ark, a gigantic floating building

2

Moshe Safdie(1938-)

The greatest satisfaction, I think, is when a building opens and
the public prossesses it and you cut the umbilical cord and you
see it taking on its own life. There's no greater satisfaction.

* 『건축가, 건축을 말하다』에서 발췌
『The Architect Says: Quotes, Quips, and Words of Wisdom』

1

1 ── 옥상정원에 이르는 과정적 공간
      the road to the rooftop garden
2 ── 공중정원의 콘크리트 기둥 숲
      this garden is a forest of concrete column

1

2

기억하다
존재 혹은 의지에 대한 상징

상징은 우리의 눈으로 볼 수 없는 의미나 가치를
구체적으로 형상화하는 것이다.
교회 건축물에 나타나는 상징은
하나님과 세상을 향한 메시지이며,
사명을 잊지 않으려는 강한 의지의 표현이다.

Remembrance:
a Symbol of our Existence or Will

A symbol embodies meanings or values that are invisible
to us. Church architecture represents the desire to send
messages to God and out to the world, and expresses the
will to uphold the mission.

1

이 우주의 디자이너가
얼마나 멋진 일을 해뒀는지 보라.
나는 차마
그 근방에도 가지 못할 것임을
너무 잘 안다.*

버크민스터 풀러(1895-1983)

1 —— 동래역 쪽에서 바라보는 진입광장과 정면
        entrance square & the front of BGVC, scenery seen from Dongrae subway station
2 —— 부산 중앙대로에서의 야경
        night view from Jungang-daero

2

Buckminster Fuller(1895-1983)

I am deeply impressed with the designer of the universe;
I am confident I couldn't have done anywhere near such a good job.

* 『건축가, 건축을 말하다』에서 발췌
『The Architect Says: Quotes, Quips, and Words of Wisdom』

바라보다
보이지 않는 그 너머를 꿈꾸며

높은 곳에 올라 먼 곳을 바라보는 것은
그 시선이 닿은 곳까지 살피고, 준비하고
떠나기 위함이다. 주변 지역은 물론 보이지 않는
지구 반대편까지.
교회는 '땅끝까지 이르러' 복음을 전하는 곳이다.
그리고 이곳은 전도자들에게 길을 잃지 않도록
빛을 비추는 등대(랜드마크)가 될 것이다.

Dreaming of and Looking Forward to an Unknown World

We climb to a high point to look at a place from a distance, looking out as far as the eye can see, in order to examine, prepare, and plan. Not only for a nearby place but also for half a world way out of sight. The church has a mission to preach the Gospel 'to the end of the world'. And this will play the role of the lighthouse that will guide the evangelists.

1

건축은 인간과 자연 사이의 끊임없는 투쟁이다.
자연을 압도하려는 투쟁,
자연을 독차지하려는 투쟁인 것이다.
건축의 제1행동강령은
돌멩이 하나를 땅 위에 두는 일이다.
이 일은 자연 상태를 문화 상태로 탈바꿈시키는 일이며,
성스러운 일이다.*

마리오 보타(1943-)

1 —— 예배동, 교육동, 기단부의 조화로운 구성
　　 harmonious composition - worship building, education building, outdoor transition zone
2 —— 온천천과 남부 부산 전경을 향해 열린 공중정원
　　 the hanging garden that open to the city and nature

2

Mario Botta(1943-)

Architecture is the constant fight between man and nature,
the fight to overwhelm nature, to possess it. The first act of
architecture is to put a stone on the ground.
That act transforms a condition of nature into a condition of
culture; it's a holy act.

* 「건축가, 건축을 말하다」에서 발췌
「The Architect Says: Quotes, Quips, and Words of Wisdom」

1

2

1 —— 대예배공간 이음홀 메인 로비
main lobby, Ieum Hall

2 —— 부산의 파노라믹한 전경을 누리는 옥외 계단
outdoor staircase with panoramic views

1

1 —— 도시와 자연을 굽어보며 오르내리는 옥외 계단
      walking and looking at the city and nature
2 —— 지하철을 통한 인한 도시와의 역동적 조우
      meet with the subway, dynamic encounter with the city

1

물이 열려 있는 대지 위로 흐르듯이,
행복도 열려 있는 삶 위로 흐른다.
문제는 이 본연의 기쁨이 흐르게 하려면
삶을 어떻게 열어야 하느냐는 것이다.*

타로 골드

1 —— 닿음아트홀 로비와 옥외 계단의 평행적 교류
        complementary transaction, lobby of Daum Art Hall & outdoor stairs.

2 —— 온천천을 향해 수평적으로 열린 이음홀 로비
        lobby of Ieum Hall. It is open to Oncheoncheon horizontally.

2

Taro Gold

As spring water rushes through open earth,
so happiness flows through open lives.
The question is how to open our lives to this inherent joy.

* 『오픈 유어 마인드』에서 발췌
『Open Your Mind, Open Your Life』, Andrews McMeel Universal(2003)

형상을 닮다, 담다
도시를 향한 몸짓과 표정

창조주가 자기 형상대로 사람을 만드신 것처럼
건축물도 만든 사람의 의지와 감정에 따라
그 모습이 달라진다. 모든 사람이 특별한 것처럼
지어진 모든 건축물도 특별하다.
저마다 다른 의미를 담고, 이웃과 도시를 향한
몸짓과 표정으로 말을 걸고 있다.

Resemble and Embrace the Image:
gesture and expressions made towards the city

Just as God created man in his own image, the appearance of architecture also depends on the will and emotions of an architect. As everyone is special, so is every building. Comprised of different meanings, each building greets its neighbours and the city with differing gestures and facades.

1

아름다움은 형태로부터 말미암는다.
그리고 전체가 몇몇 부분들과 어울리는 조응성,
또 이 부분들이 서로서로 어울리는 조응성,
또 이들이 다시 전체와 어울리는 조응성으로부터 말미암는다.
어떤 구조물이 하나의 완전하고 완벽한 덩어리로 보이려면,
그 안에서 각각의 구성물들이 서로 합치해야 하며,
그 모든 게 당신이 구현하고자 한 그 형태를 만드는 데
꼭 필요한 것이어야 한다.*

안드레아 팔라디오(1508-1580)

1 —— 온천천을 향해 빛으로 드러나는 상징적 효과, 등대와 153개 창
        lighthouse and 153 windows, symbol of light
2 —— 온천천과 도시 가로 형상에 순응하는 배치
        composition according to the shape of road and Oncheoncheon

©Choi Sang-dong

2

Andrea Palladio (1508-1580)

Beauty will result from the form and correspondence of the whole, with respect to the several parts, of the parts with regard to each other, and of these again to the whole; that the structure may appear an entire and complete body, wherein each member agrees with the other, and all are necessary to compose what you intend of form.

* 『건축가, 건축을 말하다』에서 발췌
『The Architect Says: Quotes, Quips, and Words of Wisdom』

1 — 건축을 숨 쉬게 하는 옥외 계단과 공중정원까지의 연속성
   outdoor stairs to breathe, continuity of the hanging garden
2 — 역동적 기단 위의 역동적 볼륨
   build a dynamic volume on top of a dynamic base

2

하늘을 오르다
걸어서 만나는 하늘과 땅

도시에 풍경은 수평적이기보다 수직적이다.
걸어서 이동하기 힘든 좁고 높은 공간들의 연속이다.
산을 오르듯 걸으면서 경험하는 하늘과 땅의 풍경은
매우 특별하다. 땅에서 시작된 계단으로 하늘을 향해
올라가는 것. 신자의 삶이며 인생의 교훈이다.

A Way to the Heavens:
Scaling Heaven and Earth on Foot

We may find that an urban landscape is more vertical
than horizontal. A series of narrow and high spaces that
are not good for walking continue to exist in our cities. As
you walk along, in a way similar to climbing a mountain,
you can experience a very special view of Heaven and
Earth. Going up into the sky via stairs which began at
ground level fits the journey of a Christian life and gives
us an important lesson for life.

1

길은 막힌 데가 없구나
가로막는 벽도 없고
하늘만이 푸르고 벗이고
하늘만이 길을 인도한다.
그러니
길은 영원하다.

천상병(1930-1993)

1 ── 선형으로 휘감아 오르는 옥외 계단
　　　the stairs are linearly wrapped around the building

2 ── 대예배실 로비와 통하는 옥외마당
　　　lobby of main chapel leads to the yard

2

Cheon Sang-Byeong (1930-1993)

A road is not blocked.
No wall is in the way.
Only the sky is blue and remains a friend
Only the sky leads the way
so
A road is eternal.

1

1, 2 —— 하늘을 향해 오르는 길
stairs to heaven

2

조직된 아름다움을 경험하라

BGVC는 모든 시선을 한 몸에 받는
유선형의 열린 대지 위에 있다.
길마다 새로운 도시 풍경을 경험할 수 있다.
다양한 목적으로 이곳을 찾는 모든 동선은
자연스럽게 연결되어 있고, 프로그램에 맞게
모든 공간은 잘 조직되어 움직인다.

Experience a Well-Organised Beauty

BGVC is located on the site of a streamline shape that is open and the centre of attention. Every path makes us experience the urban landscape anew. Circulations of various purposes are naturally connected all together like a flowing stream, and the well-organised spaces work properly to satisfy the programmes.

1

사랑의 랜드마크

이 공간은 지역사회를 향해 열린 크리스천 복합 문화공간이다.
현세대와 미래를 연결 지을 뿐 아니라, 부산과 태평양을 아우르며,
교회와 이웃 간에 서로 사랑을 나누는 소통의 장소로 조성되기를
기대한다. 출항하는 거대한 선박과 같이 들린 듯 열린 정면은
흔한 첨탑 형상에 기독교 건축이 머물러 있지 않고, 역동하는 장소,
자연으로 열린 공간, 도시와 교류하는 복합 건축으로 자리매김 하려는
'사랑의 띠' 조성의 의지를 드러낸다.

Landmark for love

This space is a Christian cultural complex open for the local community. We hope that it will not only connect me current generation with future generations, but also be a place of interaction that
encompasses Busan and the Pacific Ocean, and shares their love
for the church and its neighbors. The open facade, which appears
lifted like a huge departing ship, does not look like a common
Christian architecture with a spire, but reveals a positioning as
a dynamic space, open to nature, and a complex building that inter-
acts with the city.

1 —— 사랑의 랜드마크 개념을 표현한 현상설계 투시도
        perspective drawing of design competition(2011)
2 —— 평화의 랜드마크 개념을 표현한 현상설계 조감도
        perspective drawing of design competition(2011)

2

평화의 랜드마크

도심에 자연과 같은 편안한 쉼터를 제공하기 위해,
진입광장 – 옥외계단 – 공중정원 – 전망 계단 – 옥상정원에 이르는
평화로운 외부공간들이 조성된다. 마치 언덕을 오르듯
부산의 파노라믹한 전경을 교회 내외부에서 모든 시민이 즐길 수 있다.
계단 끝, 사방으로 탁트인 십자가 탑 아래 옥상정원은
그 선형 정원의 클라이맥스가 된다.

Landmark for peace

In order to provide a comfortable nature-like rest area in a peace-
ful urban outdoor space, the entrance square, outdoor stairs and
a public garden-view staircase to the rooftop garden are created.
After climbing the hill, all citizens of Busan can enjoy a panoramic
view of Busan from inside and outside the church. At the top of
the stairs, the rooftop garden under the Cross tower opens in all
directions becomes the climax of the linear garden.

1

선교의 랜드마크

세계를 향해 항해하는 선교의 방주와 같이,
어두운 바다를 밝히는 구원의 등대와 같이 지역을 중심으로
세계 선교의 비전을 품은 교회의 목표를 담는다.
어느 곳에서나 그 의미를 기억할 수 있는 상징이 된다.

Landmark for mission

BGVC is a ark for mission that sails the world. It is a lighthouse of
salvation that illuminates the dark sea. BGVC is where the vision of
world missions begins, centering on the region. It is a symbol that
can remember its meaning everywhere.

1 —— 모형, 온천천에서 바라본 모습
       model, view from Oncheoncheon
2 —— 모형 연구, 옥외 계단과 각 층 로비의 유기적 연결
       model study, organic connection between inside and outside

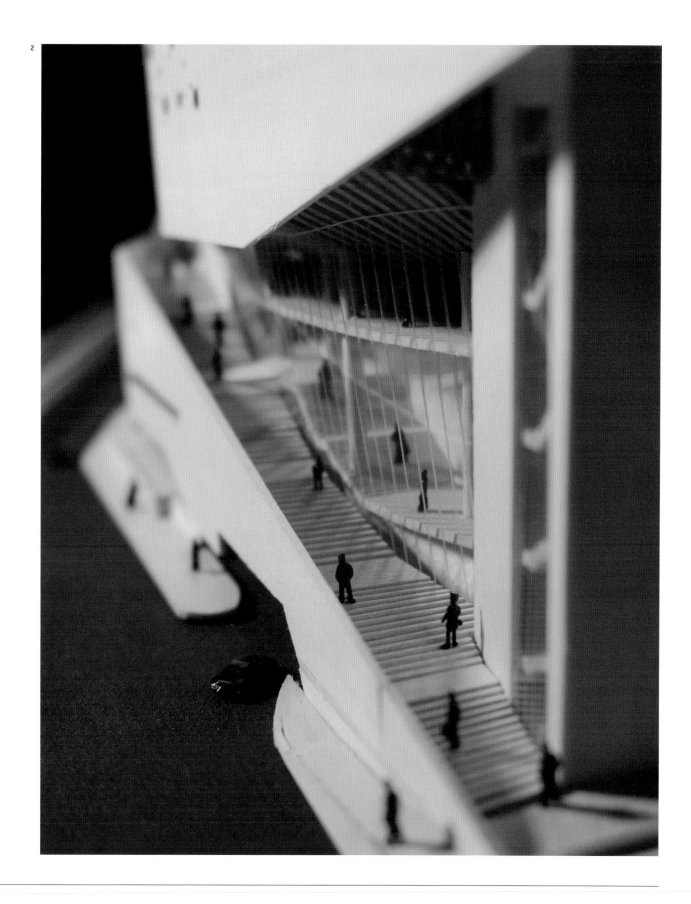

1 — Jungang-daero(50m)
2 — Oncheoncheon
3 — Busan Subway Line 1
4 — bicycle path and walking trails
5 — entrance square
6 — outdoor stage
7 — tower building
8 — sunken garden
9 — service building

site plan

0   2.5   5   10(m)

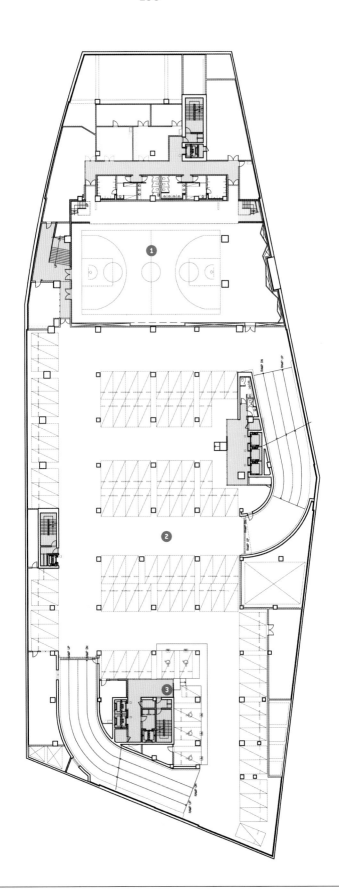

1 —— gymnasium
2 —— parking lot
3 —— hall
4 —— church school
5 —— auditorium
6 —— small theater
7 —— sunken garden

B2 plan

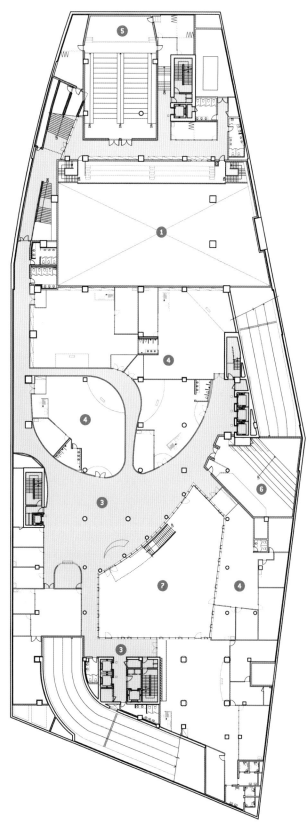

B1 plan

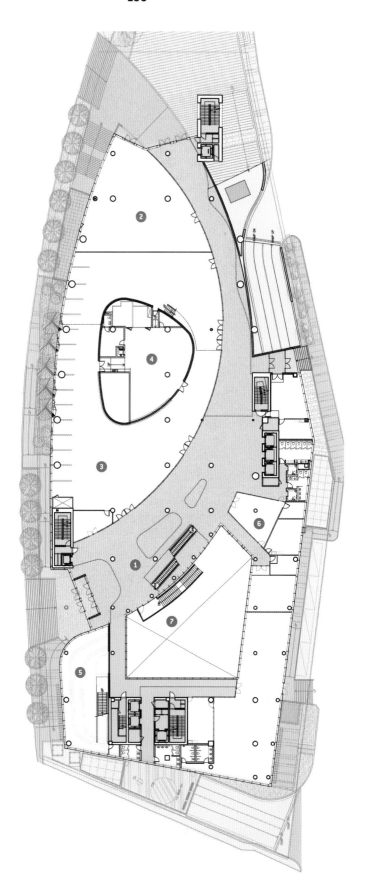

1 —— main hall·lobby
2 —— cafe
3 —— restaurant
4 —— kitchen
5 —— children's library
6 —— office
7 —— sunken garden
8 —— Daum Hall(concert hall)
9 —— gallery(multipurpose hall)
10 —— bible study room

1F plan

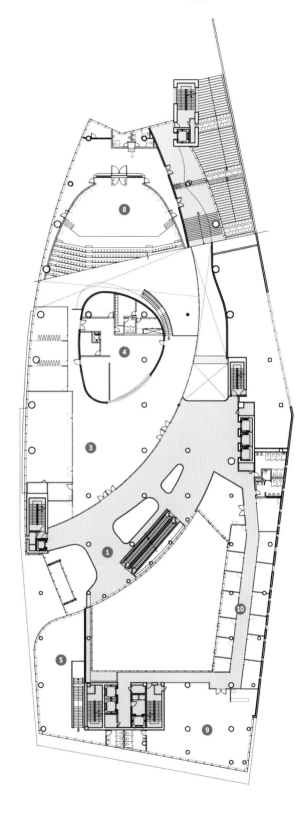

2F plan

0 2.5 5   10   20(m)

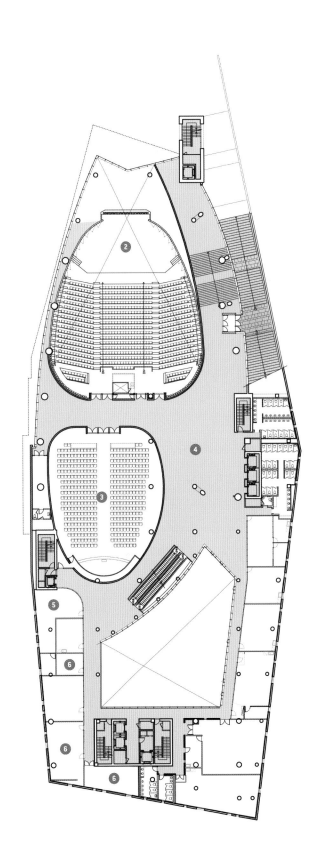

1 —— leum Hall(main chapel)
2 —— Daum Hall(concert hall)
3 —— Seum Hall(small chappel)
4 —— main hall·lobby lounge
5 —— history hall
6 —— seminar room
7 —— waiting room
8 —— choir
9 —— choir practice room
10 —— new believer's room

3F plan

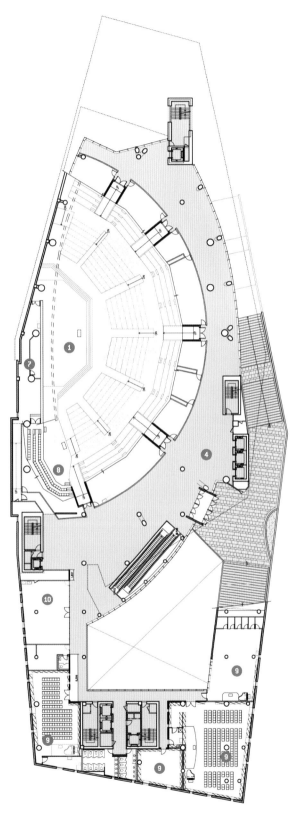

4F plan

0 2.5 5   10   20(m)

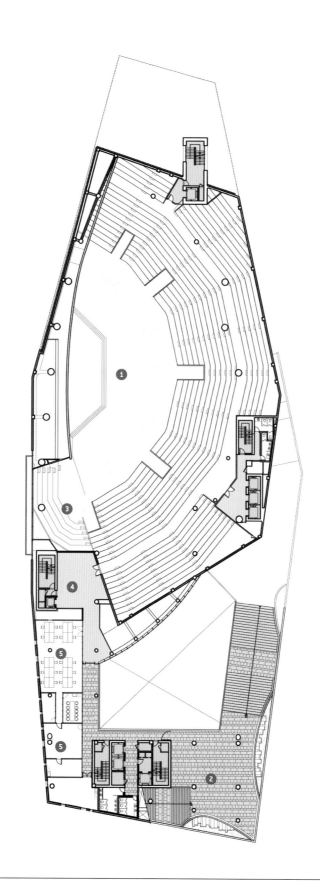

1 —— Ieum Hall(main chapel)
2 —— young square
3 —— choir
4 —— hall
5 —— religious worker's room
6 —— broadcasting booth
7 —— nursery
8 —— studio
9 —— elder's meeting room
10 —— reception room
11 —— pastor's office room

5F plan

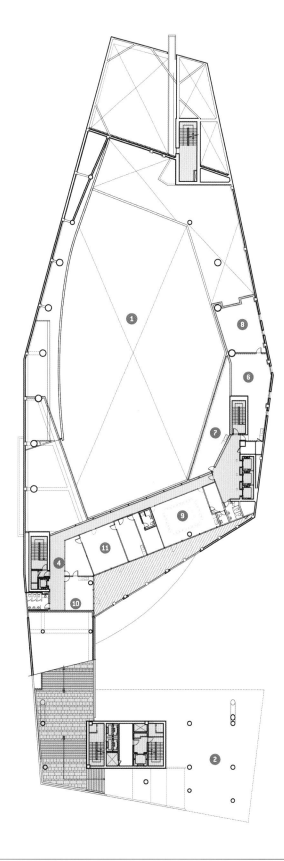

7F plan

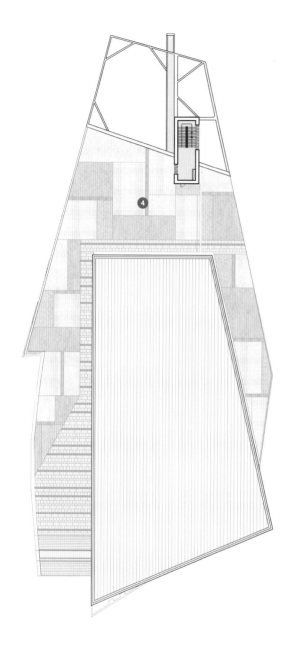

1 —— sky lounge
2 —— hall
3 —— guest room
4 —— roof garden

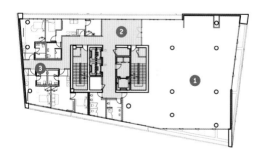

10F plan

0   2.5 5   10   20(m)

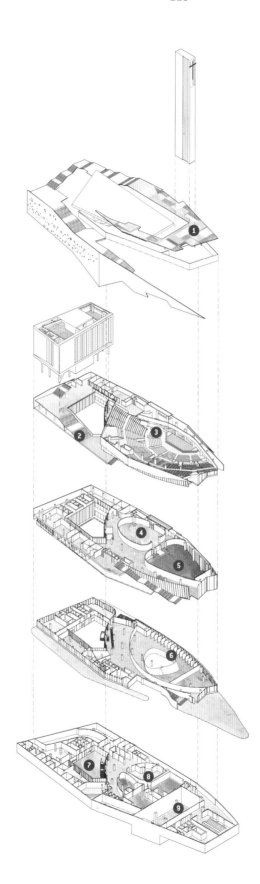

1 —— roof garden
2 —— outdoor stairs
3 —— Ieum Hall(main chapel)
4 —— Seum Hall(small chappel)
5 —— Daum Hall(concert hall)
6 —— restaurant
7 —— sunken garden
8 —— church school
9 —— gymnasium

deal drawing

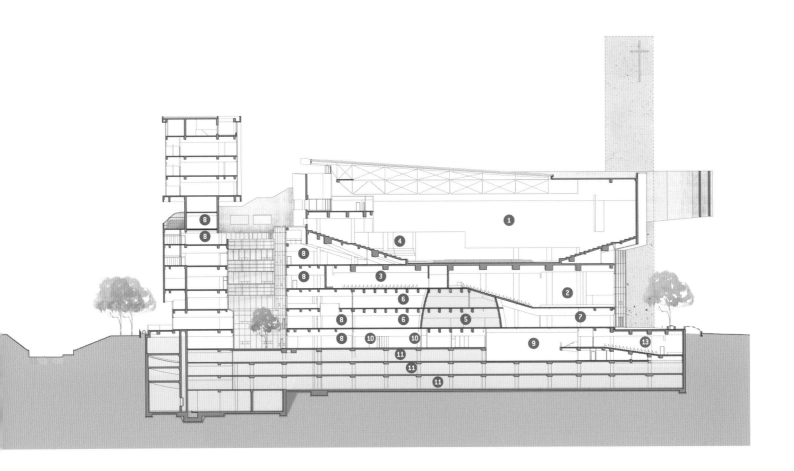

0   2.5   5   10(m)

section

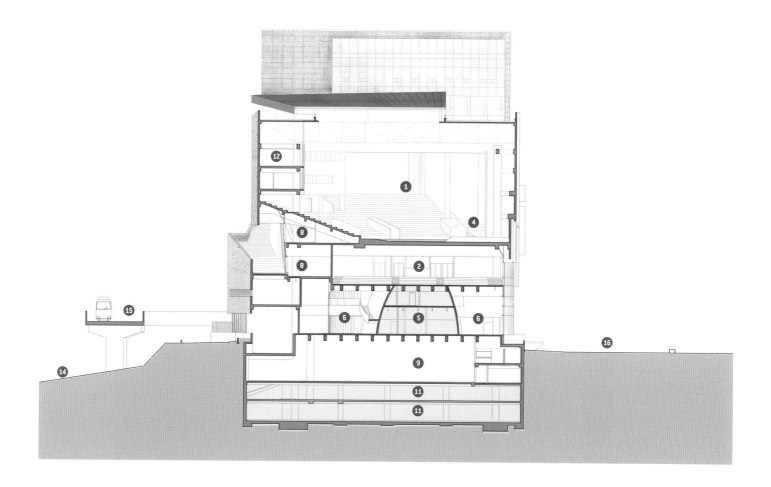

OPEN

2 PART

반석 위에
믿음을 세우다

Build faith
on the rock

극복하다
땅으로부터 자유롭기 위하여

건축물은 중력을 이기기 위해
노력한 결과이다. 오래전부터 다양한 건축 재료와
구조가 연구되었고, 인간은 중력을 극복하고 자연에
버금가는 규모의 건축물을 만들기 시작했다.
특별히 종교건축은 그 쓰임새도 물론 중요하지만,
신앙적인 경험의 장소로 저마다 마음속 기억의
장소로 남는다.

Overcome:
The Struggle to Escape the Ground

Endless struggles to escape from the force of gravity
have produced architecture. Mankind has studied various
building materials and structures for many centuries, and
have built structures that are comparable to those found
in nature by overcoming gravity. Religious architecture
should seek to impress people by devising a memorable
place and should provide us with a devotional experience,
as well as satisfying local requirements.

1

몇 십 년 전만 해도 최고의 엔지니어는
최고로 멋진 들보 혹은
구조체를 만들어낼 줄 아는 사람이었다.
오늘날 이는 대체 어찌 만들어졌는지 볼 수도
혹은 이해할 수도 없는 그런 구조를 만드는 일이 되었다.
이제 구조는 사라졌고, 당신이 얘기할 수 있는 건
오로지 색과 상징, 빛 뿐이다.
엔지니어들은 이제 기적의 미학을 구사한다.*

장 누벨(1945-)

1 —— 대예배실 공간구축 현장
       construction scene, main chapel
2 —— 대예배실 상부에 배치될 목양실과 당회실 구축 현장
       construction scene, pastor's room & conference room

2

Jean Nouvel(1945-)

The best engineer a few decades ago was someone who could create the most beautiful beam or structure; today cannot see or understand how it's done. It disappears and you can talk only about color, symbols, and light. It's an aesthetic of miracle

* 「건축가, 건축을 말하다」에서 발췌
『The Architect Says: Quotes, Quips, and Words of Wisdom』

1

모든 구조는 기초 위에 세워지고
평면이라는 대지 위에 사용된 아름다운 형태들,
형태들의 다양성, 기하학적 원리의 통일성 같은
규칙을 따라 발전해 간다.*

르 꼬르뷔지에(1887-1965)

1 — 공중정원 현장
    construction scene, the hanging garden
2 — 옥외 계단과 콘크리트 기둥 숲 현장
    construction scene, outdoor stairs and a forest of concrete column

2

Le Corbusier(1887-1965)

The whole structure rises from its base and is developed in accordance with a rule which is written on the ground in the plan: noble forms, variety of form, unity of the geometric principle.

* 「건축을 향하여」, 동녘(2002)에서 발췌
「Towards a New Architecture」

1

1 —— 드론으로 촬영한 지붕 층 공사 직전의 현장
      construction scene taken with a drone

2 —— 노출 콘크리트 캔틸레버 실현을 위한 비계 공사
      scaffolding work for cantilever construction

2

건물을 빚다
세상에서 가장 큰 조형물

콘크리트는 액화된 돌이다. 굳고 나면 돌처럼 견고한
성질이 나타나지만, 만들어지는 과정은 예술적 표현이
가능할 만큼 자유롭다. 그러나 이러한 조형성을
드러내는 만큼 치밀한 시공이 요구된다.
눈에 보이는 형상을 만들기 위해 보이지 않는
수많은 장치와 노력의 시간이 소요된다.

Creating a Building:
The Largest Sculpture in the World

Concrete is a liguid stone. It becomes as solid as stone
once it hardens, but the process is free enough to allow
for artistic expression. However, it requires precise construction as it can express such formability. It takes long
time, and a lot of devices and effort to create the chosen
shape.

©Kyungdong Construction Co. Ltd.

1

나는 특히 콘크리트가 좋다.
그건 지난 한 세기의
시공기술 진보의 상징과도 같은 것으로서,
코끼리처럼 순종적이고 강인하며,
바위처럼 기념비적이며,
벽돌처럼 소박하기까지 한 것이니까*

카를로스 빌라누에바(1900-1975)

1 —— 교육동 기준층의 기둥, 보, 바닥 거푸집 시공 현장
    construction scene, concrete formwork of education building
2 —— 드론으로 촬영한 거대 캔틸레버 상단부
    construction scene taken with a drone, upper section of cantilever

2

Carlos Villanueva(1900-1975)

I am particularly fond of concrete, symbol of the construction progress of a whole century, submissive and strong as an elephant, monumental like stone, humble like brick.

* 「건축가, 건축을 말하다」에서 발췌
『The Architect Says: Quotes, Quips, and Words of Wisdom』

1 — 연암 발파를 위한 천공 현장
boring for soft rock blasting

2 — 연암 발파를 위한 폭약 설치 현장
Install explosives for soft rock blasting

3 — 기초 및 지하층 바닥 공사
lay the foundations of BGVC

3

드러내다
있는 그대로. 숨기지 않고

현대인은 속내를 드러내지 않는다.
경계심 때문이다. 마찬가지로 재료의 성질도
겉으로 드러내지 않게 되었다.
콘크리트조 건물에 돌과 철판을 붙이고,
벽돌로 지은 집에 페인트를 칠하기도 한다.
근본이 어떤 재료인지 알려주기보다는
꾸미는 일에 치중한다.
노출 콘크리트는 꾸미지 않고 속살을 그대로 드러낸다.
처음 만들어진 상태 그대로 솔직하고 담대하다.
날것이다.

Without Hiding, as it is

Nowadays, people hardly express what's on their mind because they are wary of the response of others. They don't always reveal the true nature of a building material either. Concrete buildings are finished with stone and iron plates, and brick houses are often daubed with paint. Instead of disclosing the original material of the building, they focus on decoration. Exposed concrete does not ornament a surface but reveals its bare skin. It is simple and bold, in the way it is made. It is raw.

1

1 —— 연속적으로 내외부 공간을 관통하게 하는 보도형 로비
       corridor lobby, the visitor pass through BGVC comfortably

2 —— 원활한 출입을 배려한 바닥 재료의 모색
       continuous internal flooring material from outside

우리 작업은 이 세계를
보다 이해 가능하게 하는 것이어야지
그것을 더 혼돈스럽게 해서는 안된다.
나무 같이 보이는 건 나무여야만 하며,
쇠는 쇠붙이로 머물러야 한다.*

권터 베니쉬(1922-2010)

We shoul work on making our world understana-
ble and not make it more confused. What looks
like wood should also be wood and iron should
remain iron.

Gunter Behnisch(1922-2010)

2

* 「건축가, 건축을 말하다」에서 발췌
「The Architect Says: Quotes, Quips, and Words of Wisdom」

1 —— 사전 테스트 결과물을 보존하여 진입 광장 야외무대로 활용
       the mock-up was used as an outdoor stage
2 —— 고품질 노출 콘크리트 시공을 위한 사전 테스트
       exposed concrete test construction case

건축의 본질은 여러분이 행하는
선택의 질과 정신력에 달려 있지,
값비싼 재료나 대리석 또는
희귀한 목재의 활용에 있지 않다.*

르 꼬르뷔지에(1887-1965)

And that you realize that this essence of architecture is in the quality of your choice in the
force of your spirit and at all in rich materials, in
marble or rare wood.

Le Corbusier(1887-1965)

2

* 『프레시지옹』, 동녘(2004)에서 발췌
『Precisions on the Present State of Architecture and City Planning』

1

1 —— **노출 콘크리트 거푸집 외부 시공 상세**
   exposed concrete formwork external construction detail

2 —— **노출 콘크리트 거푸집 내측 시공 상세**
   exposed concrete formwork internal construction detail

3 —— **거푸집 제거 직후, 노출 콘크리트 면**
   exposed concrete surface after removal of formwork

결과는 볼 수 없는 과정의 일부분

어떤 시간을 거쳐 만들어졌는지 알지 못하면
그 모습을 제대로 평가할 수 없을 것이다.
기록은 볼 수 없는 비밀의 시간을 알려준다.
공사의 과정은 과거가 아닌 현재의 모습이다.

Part of a Process that Doesn't Show the Results

If you do not know the time that has passed, you can't appreciate it properly. A record informs of us an unrevealed time. Records of a construction process are not the past but in the present.

1

건설현장은 건축가에게 놀랍도록 큰 가르침을 주는 장소다.
내게 선택권을 준다면 난 단번에 로마의 성 베드로 성당 건물
공사현장으로 달려가 거기서 한 시간을 보내는 편을 택할 것이다.
그 성당에 대해 쓴 모든 책들을 다 읽는 것보다 말이다.*

요른 웃손(1918-2008)

1 —— 경사 바닥 실현을 위한 철골조 시공 현장
        construction of steel structure for inclined slab

2 —— 예배동의 징크마감 지붕 공사
        roofing work of worship building, zinc finishinge

©Kyungdong Construction Co.,Ltd.

2

Jorn Utzon(1918-2008)

A construction site is an incredibly instructive place for an architect. I would rather have spent an hour at the Saint Peter's building site in Rome than have read all the books written about that church.

* 「건축가, 건축을 말하다」에서 발췌
「The Architect Says: Quotes, Quips, and Words of Wisdom」

1

대지의 법칙으로 인해, 건축은 자의적 독단에 빠지지 않고
원칙과 형태, 그리고 통일된 전체를 찾을 수 있다.
건축 기술은 자연으로부터의 문화적 소외가 아니라
인간과 주변의 환경 사이에 관계를 만드는 일이다.*

르 꼬르뷔지에(1887-1965)

1 —— 타원형 대예배실의 계단형 회중석 시공
　　　construction scene, tier of seats in main chapel
2 —— 대예배실 장의자 설치 현장
　　　installation scene, pews of main chapel

2

Le Corbusier(1887-1965),

Due to the Law for the Land, architecture will once again find a principle, a form and a unity free of arbitrary dogma. Technology is not a cultural alienation from nature, but the establishment of contact between man and his environment.

* 「르 꼬르뷔지에 학생들과의 대화」, 엠지에이치엔드맥그로우한(2000)에서 발췌
　「Le Corbusier Talks with Students」

1

1 —— 비계를 제거함과 동시에 윤곽을 드러내는 캔틸레버
the scaffold is removed and the outline of the cantilever is revealed

2 —— 비계 철거 현장의 아침
a morning scene, removal of scaffolding

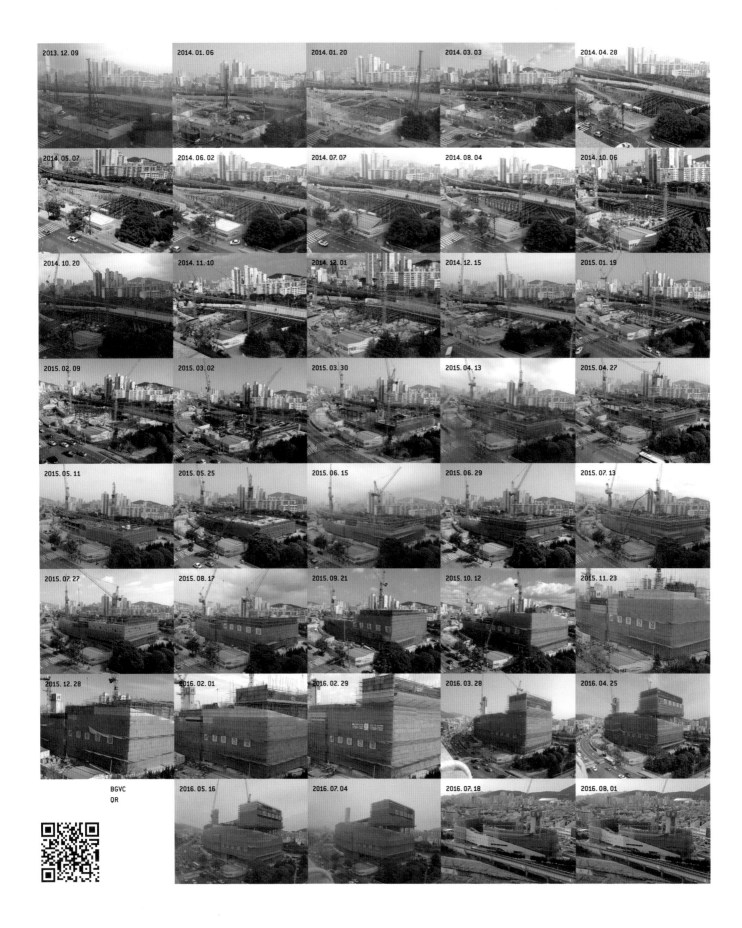

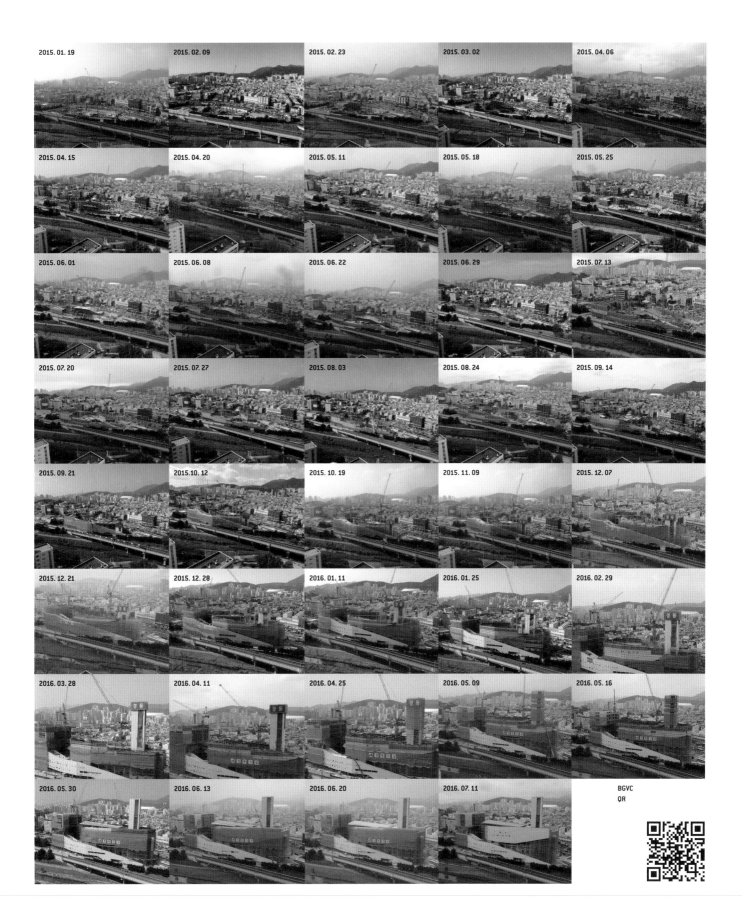

OPEN

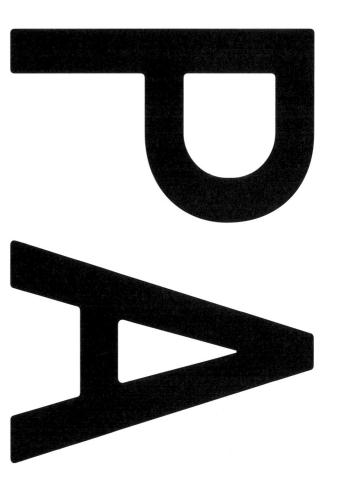

3 PART

세상을 향해
열리다

Open
to the world

살아있는 것은 늘 변화한다

긴 역사의 공동체일수록 변화를 인정하는 일은 어렵다.
긴 세월의 기억만큼 변화는 낯설고 부정적일 수 있다.
이스라엘 민족의 출애굽 사건은 혁신을 위한
움직임이었다. 언약을 기억하고 약속의 땅으로 움직일 때
비로소 새로운 역사가 시작되었다.

Living Creatures Always Change

Historical communities typically find it more difficult
to accept change. The longer the history of their collec-
tive memory, the stranger and more negative change
will seem. The Exodus of the Israelites was a move for
change. A new history could begin only when they re-
membered the covenant and moved to the Promised
Land.

1

나는 너를 애굽 땅에서 인도하여 낸 여호와 네 하나님이니   시편 81:10
네 입을 크게 열라 내가 채우리라 하였으나

1 —— 소예배실(세움홀) 로비
       lobby of small chapel(Seum Hall)
2 —— 중층 높이를 활용한 주 출입구의 환대 효과
       the ceiling of lobby is high to provide comfort

2

Psalms 81:10

I am the LORD your God, who brought you up out of Egypt.
open wide your mouth and I will fill it.

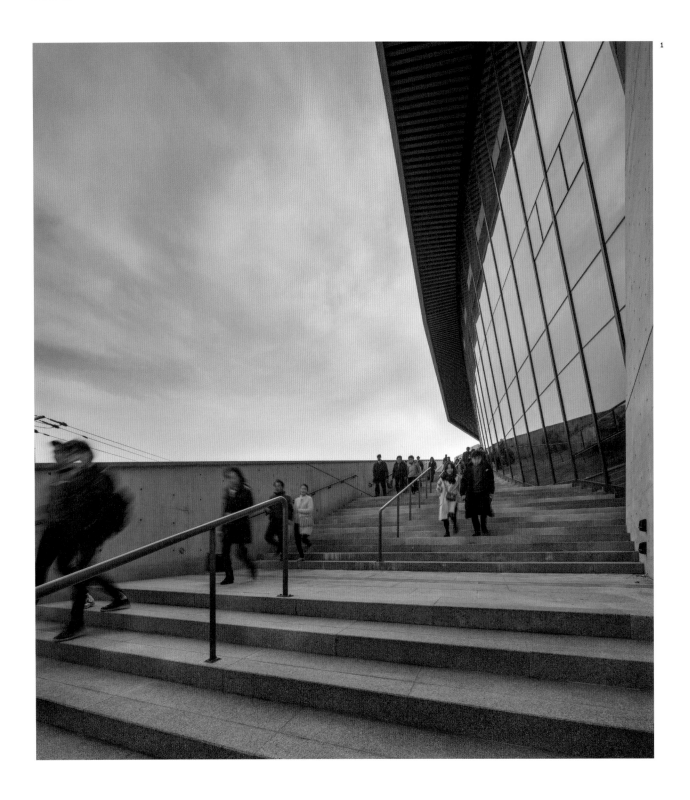

1 —— 하늘과 땅의 만남을 연출하는 옥외 계단
    outdoor stairs, heaven and earth meet

2 —— 골조완성과 함께 드러난 공간의 실용적 형상
    after frame work, the utility of the space has been revealed

충만한 가운데 세계를 보다

BGVC는 지역과 세계를 모두 담기 위한 그릇이다.
세계선교의 비전만 바라보고 지역을 돌아보지 못한
유럽 교회의 어려움을 거울삼아
부산에 대한 비전을 먼저 생각했다.
교회의 비전을 세운 후에 건축을 결정하였다.
그 안을 가득 채우고, 지역과 세계를 향한
항해를 준비하고 있다.

Looking at a World Filled with God's Grace

BGVC is a container that is both local and global. Learning lessons from the mistakes of European churches, which paid closer attention to a world mission rather than accounting for their local residents, I came up with a vision for Busan. Instead of devising a vision for architecture, I decided on the construction after establishing a vision for the church. First, I made my church, and now I am preparing for a local and global voyage.

1

건축은 공간을 체계적으로 구성하는 일이며,
교회 건축은 예배를 위한 공간들을 체계적으로 구성하는 일이다.
한 공동체의 예배를 위한 공간을 구성하는 일을 돕는 건축가는
반드시 그 공동체의 예배에 관한 모든 정보를 받아야 한다.
이처럼 교회 건축에 대한 논의는 항상 이 공간으로 의도하는
기능에 대한 질문들로부터 시작한다.
"여기서 우리는 무엇을 하려고 하는가?"*

제임스 화이트 · 수잔 화이트

1 —— 닿음아트홀 음악회
        concert in Daum Art Hall
2 —— 대예배실에서의 집회 전경
        scene of worship in main chapel(Ieum Hall)

2

James F. White & Susan J. White

Architecture is the organization of space, and church architecture is the organization of spaces for worship. The architect who helps a community organize space for worship must receive thorough information about what the community does in its worship. Thus we always begin a discussion of church architecture with questions about the intended function of this space. "What do we do here?"

* 「교회 건축과 예배 공간」에서 발췌

『Church Architecture』

1 —— 공사현장 방문 기도
visit to pray at construction site

2 —— 골조완성 감사예배
worship, completion of structure BGVC

3 —— 온천천의 새로운 풍경
new scenery of Oncheoncheon

3

1

음악은 흐르는 건축이며, 건축은 동결된 음악이다.   괴테(1749-1832)

1 ── 닿음아트홀 전경
       Daum Art Hall
2 ── 소예배실(세움홀)의 율동적 실내 공간
       the rhythm of space, small chapel(Seum Hall)

2

Johann Wolfgang von Goethe(1749-1832)

Music is liquid architecture; Architecture is frozen music.

공공 공간에 대한 가능성

교회가 지역사회를 위한 공공 공간으로
역할을 할 수 있으려면 문을 활짝 열고,
가장 편안한 얼굴로 반겨야 한다.
소유가 아닌 공유의 장소로 인식되는 순간,
친밀하게 이웃과 대화를 나눌 수 있다.

Possibilities for Public Spaces

A church must welcome people to serve as a public space for the community, with their doors open wide and with the most comfortable face. As soon as it is recognised as a place that is shared rather than owned, it will be able to greet to members as close neighbours.

1

어떤 집, 어떤 교회 혹은 궁전의 정면과 벽들은
그게 아무리 아름답다 하더라도 그저 용기일 뿐이다.
벽에 둘러싸인 상자일 뿐이라는 말이다.
중요한 콘텐츠는 그 내부공간이다.*

브루노 제비(1918-2000)

1 — 건축 전체를 숨 쉬게 하는 중앙 선큰 전경
      sunken space, passage of light and wind
2 — 지하 1층 주일학교 공간과 연계된 선큰의 활용
      a church school located in the basement is connected to sunken space

©Choi Sang-dong

2

Bruno Zevi(1918-2000)

The facade and walls of a house, church, or palace, no matter how beautiful they may be, are only the container, the box formed by the walls; the content is the internal space.

* 『건축가, 건축을 말하다』에서 발췌
『The Architect Says: Quotes, Quips, and Words of Wisdom』

1 —— 어린이 도서관의 도심 속 독서 풍경
        children can read in the library comfortably

2 —— 도시에 녹아든 듯, 온천천에 떠 있는 BGVC
        BGVC floating on the Oncheoncheon

2

생명
지속가능한 공간의 조건

이 땅의 모든 '지속가능성'은 생명력을 기준으로 한다.
시간이 지나도 그 움직임이 한결같은
지속가능한 공간이 되려면 '살아있는' 인자들이
서로를 깨우는 일을 멈추지 말아야 한다.
마치 연쇄 반응이 이어지는 것처럼 서로에게 생명력을
전하는 건강한 공동체의 움직임이 필요하다.

Life:
Conditions for Sustainable Space

The whole of 'sustainability' is always based on vitality.
A sustainable space engaged with constant movement
over time requires 'living' factors to keep waking along
with each other. Healthy communities should move, ex-
changing their vitality each other like a chain reaction.

©Pixelhouse

1

모든 전통의 그리스도인들은, '참여'를 그 건축의 공간적
배열을 포함하여 예배에 관한 모든 것을 평가하는 핵심적인 기준으로
사용해왔다. 미래에는 참여가 지금보다 훨씬 더 광범위한 의미를
가지게 될 것이다. 공간이라는 측면에서 '참여'를 다른 말로
표현한다면, 그것은 공간이 주는 친밀감이다.*

제임스 화이트·수잔 화이트

1 —— 다채로운 아지트 공간으로 조성된 어린이 도서관
    children's library, composition in various spaces
2 —— 다목적 프로그램을 수용할 체육관
    gymnasium, multipurpose space

2

James F. White & Susan J. White

Christians of every tradition have used 'participation' as a key criterion for evaluating everything about worship, including its architectural setting. As we look to the future, participation may have even broader meaning than we now realize.

* 『교회 건축과 예배 공간』에서 발췌
　『Church Architecture』

함께 누린다는 것
햇빛처럼, 단비처럼 모두에게 축복을

좋은 것은 함께 누릴수록 좋다.
자연의 모든 것이 그렇듯 좋은 공간은
함께 할 수 있을 때 더 좋다. 교회를 통해 이 사회가
유익할 수 있도록, 삶의 활력이 넘칠 수 있도록,
하늘의 복이 흘러넘칠 수 있도록.

Enjoying Together:
A Blessing for Everyone like Sunlight and Welcome Rain

The more we share good things, the better they will be.
Like everything in nature, a good space becomes better
when you share it between everyone. I hope the church
will contribute to our society, to make our life full of vitality, and to pray for God's blessings.

1

반석을 여신즉 물이 흘러나와
마른 땅에 강 같이 흘렀으니

시편 105:41

1 —— 옥외마당에서의 잔치
      outdoor garden party
2 —— 주일 구내식당 활용
      operate a cafeteria on sunday

©Choi Sang-dong

2

Psalms 105:41

He opened the rock, and water gushed out;
like a river it flowed in the desert.

1, 2, 3 ⎯ 다음 세대들의 다양한 공간 활용
well-used spaces for a new generation

신앙의 본질을 향한 건축적 형상화

이은석 × 이관석

Q. 이관석. **오랜 기간 성심을 다해 작업해오던 BGVC가 완공된 것을 축하드린다. 이 교수님이 교회당을 설계해 처음 완공시킨 해가 몇 년도이고 BGVC가 준공된 교회로서 몇 번째인가?**

A. 이은석. 교회 건축에 관한 내 기록을 보니 2000년에 대전 유성의 100평 땅에 목양교회를 준공한 것이 처음이었다. 새로운 세기가 시작된 2000년은 건축가 이력에 매우 중요한 해였다. 그 해에 '천년의 문' 현상설계에 당선되었고 나의 첫 교회 작품인 목양교회도 마무리했다.

또한 나의 건축 디자인에서 지금도 여전히 가장 소중한 가치로 보듬고 있는 'Minimum'에 대한 철학이 실무를 통해서 확인되고 확신을 갖게 된 시기도 그 즈음이었다. 부전글로컬비전센터가 몇 번째 예배당인지는 정확히 세어봐야 알겠지만, 신축 예배당 숫자만 따져도 100개는 훌쩍 넘을 것 같다.

Q. 이관석. **불과 17년 동안에 한국의 역대 건축가 중에서 교회 건물을 가장 많이 설계해 완성시켰고, 세계적으로 봐서도 그럴 것 같다. 우연은 아닐 텐데, 자신의 어떤 면이 그런 기회를 가져왔다고 생각하나?**

A. 이은석. 20세기말 한국의 교회 건축계는 모더니즘적 실용성과 경제적이고 절제된 형태 미학을 갈구하고 있었다. 그래서 모더니즘 정신으로 건축 실무를 막 시작한 내게 개신교 예배당 건축설계의 기회가 많이 온 것 같다. 건축적으로나 삶의 태도로 볼 때 나는 전형적인 모더니스트다. 나는 독실한 개신교도 가정문화 속에서, 청교도적이라 할 만큼 절제된 칼뱅주의적 삶을 요구받는 가정환경에서 자랐다.

나의 건축적 사고가 정립된 유학시절 프랑스 파리

도 모더니즘과 진보적인 아방가르드적 예술철학으로 가득한 분위기였다. 프랑스는 가톨릭의 나라이기는 하지만 칼뱅이 태어나 활동하던 나라여서인지 모든 분야가 진보적이었다. 사회 전반과 문화적으로 개신교적 경향의 철학과 일맥상통하는 프렌치 모던 미학이 융성했다. 이러한 나의 성장배경을 바탕으로 유럽의 모더니즘적 건축 분위기를 강하게 경험하고 귀국한 내가 처음 접하게 된 1990년대 후반 한국의 교회 건축 분야는 물량으로는 엄청나게 많았으나 상대적으로 포스트모던(post-modern)적이었고 미학적으로는 형태주의(formalism)에 함몰되어 건축적으로 극한 빈곤에 처해 있었다. 지금 돌아보면 그 스타일이 좀 우습기까지 한 강남의 충현교회나 광림교회, 대구의 제일교회 등은 마치 중세 고딕성당을 흉내 내는 것이 신앙의 보수성과 경건함을 유지하는 태도라고 착각한 듯하다.

이 당시 고딕성당의 변형인 경동교회도 지어졌지만, 그 역시 조형성에 집중됐다. 이처럼 한국의 교회 건축은 무개념·무방비 상태에서 1980-90년대를 보내고 있었다. 이러한 상황에서 당시 내가 진보적이고 모더니즘적인 교회 건축 개념을 살짝 제시했을 뿐인데, 신축을 원하는 많은 교회와 교계 지도자들이 나의 견해에 공감하며 당시 드물었던 모던한 교회 건축가인 내게 뜻밖의 성원을 해주신 것이다. 그 당시 목회 저널에 꾸준히 새로운 교회 건축을 하기 위한 자세에 대해 연재를 했었다. 그것들을 묶어서 도발적 제목의 단행본 『새로운 교회 건축 이렇게 하라』를 두란노서원에서 발간했다. 전국을 다니며 교회 건축에 대해 많이 강연했고, 라디오와 TV 방송에도 교회 건축과 관련해서 출연하기도 했다.

Q. 이관석. **어릴 때부터 신앙생활을 하면서 지금까지 여러 교회를 다녔고, 건축을 연구하며 다수의 국내 종교 건축물들을 답**

L —— 이관석
Lee Kwan-seok
Professor,
Department of Architecture,
Kyung Hee University

R —— 이은석
Lee Eun-seok
Architect of Atelier KOMA,
Professor of DAKHU

사하기도 했다. 앞서 비교적 가까운 과거인 1990년대 후반 한국 교회 건축에 대한 언급이 있었는데, 한국의 근대 이후 개신교 건축의 변화에 대해 숙고하신 바를 좀 더 개진한다면?

A. 이은석. 서구의 경우, 종교의 다원화와 모든 기독교 교회를 교파와 교회의 차이를 넘어 하나로 통일시키고자 하는 진보적 기독교 신학 운동인 에큐메니컬(Ecumenical) 운동이 보편화되면서 신·구교 구분할 수 없을 정도로 예배당 공간이 차별 없이 사용되는 것을 보고 있다. 그러나 개신교적 실용성과 미학적 단순성이 세계 건축에서 각광받게 된 것은 독일의 사회학자 막스 베버(Max Weber)가 정리한 '프로테스탄트 윤리와 자본주의 정신(Protestant Ethic and the Spirit of Capitalism)'의 영향이 지대했다고 본다.

이러한 철학이 뒷받침되어 일상의 건축적 미학이 경건하고 성스러운 건축의 자리로 대체된 것이다. 하지만 한국 개신교 교회는 세계사의 흐름에 비해 훨씬 늦게 건축에 대한 고민을 하게 됐다고 본다. 한국적인 개신교 교회의 변혁은 1974년에 여의도광장을 중심으로 열렸던 'Expolo 74'라는 대규모 집회를 중심으로 일어났다고 개인적으로는 생각한다. 이 시기 이후에 개신교 내에서도 교단의 벽이 허물어지기 시작했고, 교회가 한국 사회를 향해 선교의 자신감을 갖기 시작했다고 볼 수 있다.

이 양적 부흥의 시기에 한국 교회 건축에서 뚜렷이 드러나는 외형주의와 물량주의의 흔적을 찾을 수 있다. 이즈음 교회가 많은 신자를 수용하기 위해 예배실의 발코니와 부채꼴의 평면 형식을 창안해낸 듯하다. 하지만 부채꼴 예배실 형식은 말씀 중심으로 목회자에게만 집중하게 하는 약점이 있다. 발코니석의 존재는 예배 속에서 한 공동체를 조성하는 데 방해가 되기도 했다. 최근 들어 교회의 양적 성장이 둔화되고

예배와 교제의 깊이를 요구하는 경향에서는, 다행스럽게도 보다 낮고 넓고 편편하게 무대화된 강단과 하나의 공동체 의식을 지원하는 단층의 예배실로 건축하는 교회가 증가되는 추세이다.

Q. 이관석. 한국 기독교 건축에 대한 그런 이해가 지금의 부전 교회 건축을 낳았을 것이다. 이에 대해 곧 다시 얘기하기로 하고, 그보다 먼저 지금까지 본 종교건물 중 가장 기억에 남는 것은 무엇인지 궁금하다. 이 교수님의 교회 건축 계획에도 영향을 미쳤을 텐데.

A. 이은석. 내게 가장 기억에 남는 종교 건축은, 짐작하겠지만 역시 르 꼬르뷔지에(Le Corbusier)의 롱샹성당이다. 가톨릭의 순례자 성당이어서 개신교 교회의 기능과 직접적인 연관성을 찾기는 어렵지만, 교회 건축이 그 흔한 고딕의 수직적이고 랜드마크적인 정서로부터 자유하고 있다는 사실, 추상적 미학의 가치로 독창적 종교건축의 형상을 제시한 점, 전승을 완전히 새롭게 재창조한 시도 등에서 롱샹성당이 가장 기억에 남는 종교건축일 수밖에 없다. 특히 보일 듯 말 듯한 철봉으로 만들어져 돔 위에 살짝 꽂힌 작은 십자가는 사뭇 충격적이었다. 우리 국내의 일반적 정서로는 그 건물의 생김새와 무관하게 눈에 띄게 붉고 거대한 네온사인 발광체의 십자가를 꽂아야 교회당인 줄 알았는데 말이다.

당시 내가 느낀 감상은 우리네 교회 건축의 현실과는 너무 대조되는, 일종의 비타민과 같은 효과였다. 그처럼 상징의 효과는 크기가 아니라 대비에 있었다. 이런 여러 가지 르 꼬르뷔지에의 건축적 태도가 건축 공부를 시작하던 내게 너무나 신선하게 다가왔었다.

그 이후에 단순함과 검소함, 추상적 공간의 가치를

Conversation.

신앙의 본질을 향한 건축적 형상화
an architectural manifestation of the essence of faith

198

이은석 × 이관석
Lee Eun-seok × Lee Kwan-seok

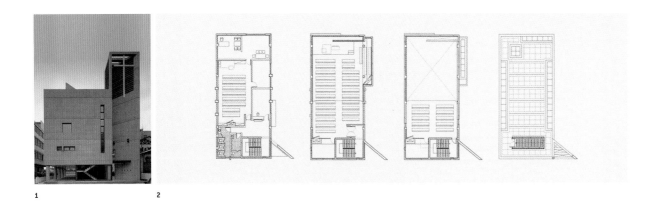

1   2

예배당에서 보여준 라투레트 수도원에서의 추억도 빼놓을 수 없다. 또한 오랜 세월 미완의 프로젝트로 묻혀 있다가 최근에 뒤늦게 완성되며 다시 빛을 보게 된 피르미니의 교회는 중년이 된 건축가인 내게도 감동적이었다. 거기서는 건축에서 조형, 공간, 시간을 담는 일에 근원적인 실험을 해냈고, 마치 우주선처럼, 그간 인류가 단 한 번도 보지 못했던 공간을 품은 신비한 물체를 디자인해내지 않았는가? 최근에 현상학을 논하고 브루탈리즘적 가치가 우리 시대 건축에서는 마치 새로운 것인 양 과장되며 재조명되고 있지만, 그는 이미 50-60년 전에 그런 건축적 시도를 다 해 버렸다. 르 꼬르뷔지에와 같은 대선배가 먼저 지나갔다는 사실이 후대 건축가인 우리가 이 땅에 착지하는 데 너무나 큰 도움이 된다.

Q. 이관석. **감동으로서의 건축이 이룰 수 있는 놀라운 성취를 보여준 롱샹 성당과 라투레트 수도원이 주는 교훈은 시공을 초월해 여전한 것 같다. 이 교수님은 교회당을 '신앙의 본질을 향한 건축적 형상화'로 이해한다. 현대 교회 건축이 지향해야 할 '개신교에서의 신앙의 본질'에 대해 어떻게 생각하는가.**

A. 이은석. 마가의 다락방에서부터 초대 교회 기독교 핍박 시기의 카타콤이나 중세의 거대한 성당을 거쳐 현대 미국의 체육관에 이르기까지 기독교 공동체는 언제나 함께 예배드리기 위해 모일 장소가 필요했다. 그리스도인은 예배를 위해 모일 때 그 가운데 임재하시는 하나님을 체험한다. 그런 점에서 볼 때, 나는 여는 행위와 모으는 행위를 물리적 공간으로 조성하는 일이 교회 건축의 우선된 목적이라 생각해 왔다. 기독교 신앙이 궁극적으로 지향하는 바는 무형의 교회겠지만 건축행위에서는 유형화할 수 있는 어떤 가치가 필요하게 된다. 그것은 모든 세대의 교회 건축 작업에서 고민해 온, 즉 공간을 활짝 여는 것과 함께 모이는 장소(gathering space)를 조성해 가기 위한 방안들이다.

그러므로 교회 건축에서 기념비적 효과나 장식적인 형상만을 추구하는 것은 본질에 대한 접근이 아니다. 선교를 위해 문을 넓게 여는 일, 공동체의 예배를 위해 여러 갈래 길로부터 한 장소로 모이게 하는 일이 바로 교회 건축의 핵심이며, 교회 건축 작업에 임하는 본질적 태도라고 본다. 희랍어로 교회는 에클레시아(ekklesia), 즉 모이도록 부름 받았다(called out)는 의미를 갖고 있다. 모이는 것이 교회됨의 필수인 만큼 교회 건축은 모으는 기능이 효과적으로 작동하여 공동체가 잘 예배하게 하는 일일 것이다.

Q. 이관석. **그런 전통적이고 불변하는 성결적 신앙을 지키고 나누며 전파하는 장소인 교회당이 현대 문화가 요구하는 기능을 수용하고 그에 맞는 새로운 미학을 찾으면서 건축적 형상화는 상당히 다른 결과물을 갖고 왔다. 이런 관점에서 현대 개신교 건축을 보며 느낀 가장 큰 고민은 무엇인가?**

A. 이은석. 상징이 건축 본질의 일부임을 부인할 수는 없겠지만, 우리가 도시나 전원에서 쉽사리 접하게 되는 현란하고 거대한 십자가가 달린, 과도하게 기념적이거나 특이한 형상을 지닌 교회당을 볼 때, 그 교회당은 본질보다는 상업적인 간판 기능만을 추구하는 것으로 여겨진다. 마치 로버트 벤추리의 장식된 쉐드(the decorated shed)처럼 돼 버리는 것이다.

스스로 비정상적이란 사실을 알면서도 재정 상황을 비롯한 여러 이유에서 그러한 불균형의 교회당 건물을 어쩔 수 없이 수용할 수밖에 없는 공동체도 물론 있을 것이다. 하지만 충분한 재정 여유를 가졌음에도 불균형에 빠져 있는 경우를 보면,

1 —— 목양교회 정면
       facade of Mokyang Church
2 —— 목양교회의 단순명료한 평면
       plain and simple plan of Mokyang Church
3 —— 푸른마을교회의 단순, 검소, 추상
       Green Village Church: simple, frugal, abstract

3

너무나 세속적이고 상업적이라고밖에 생각할 수 없는 교회당들이 오늘날 한국에서는 범람하고 있다. 건축의 껍질에만 관심을 가진 태도인데, 심지어는 그 껍질조차도 균형 있게 만들지 못하는 것이 안타깝다는 것이다.

Q. 이관석. 그런 각성이 오늘날 한국 교회가 극복해야 할 모습으로서 이 교수님이 다수의 교회 건물을 설계하는 데 바탕이 됐을 것 같다. 부전교회에서도 마찬가지였을 것이다. BGVC설계에 바탕이 된 건축 개념을 간략하게 설명한다면?

A. 이은석. 아직도 표피적이고 형태주의적인 면에 함몰된 채 지어지고 있는 한국의 숱한 교회당을 보면서, 교회 설계를 진행하며 형태와 상징 그 자체에만 빠지지 않도록 스스로 제어하는 데에 필요한 기술 한두 가지를 내게 제시하라고 한다면, 나는 추상적 공간 가치 유발에 집중하라고 말하고 싶다.

대규모인 부전교회 프로젝트를 시작하면서 달성하고자 한 가치는 첫째로 들린 구조로부터 유발되는 열린 가치의 상징(선교적 랜드마크), 두 번째로는 건축의 연속적 제스처가 조성하는 교회와 도시와 이웃과의 소통(사랑의 랜드마크), 세 번째로는 기회가 생길 때마다 곳곳에 조성하려는 안식의 공간으로서 녹지 정원과 데크(평화의 랜드마크)를 들 수 있다. 이 세 가지 공간의 개념적 목표가 부전교회당에서의 주요 설계 개념이 된 것이다. 앞으로 설계하는 다른 교회에서도 공히 적용될 가치라고 본다.

Q. 이관석. 그 개념에는 부전교회의 목회 철학과 비전, 대지 조건을 포함한 땅과의 교감, 초대형 규모에 대응할 논리 등 여러 가지 요인이 반영됐을 것이다. 교회의 목회 철학과 비전이 내포됐을 공간 프로그램을 처음 대했을 때 어떤 생각이 들었나? 그

리고 BGVC는 이 교수님이 지금까지 계획한 어느 교회 건물보다 크다. 규모 차이로 인해 지금까지와는 다른 시도를 의무적으로 또는 희망적으로 시도한 것이 있는가?

A. 이은석. BGVC는 그 명칭에서 보듯이 국제적이고도 동시에 지역적이기를 원하는 데서부터 시작됐다. 더 넓은 세계를 향한 선교적 태도는 대부분의 교회가 지향하는 바이긴 하다. 하지만 BGVC 건축에 따른 이 교회의 목회 철학은 상당히 달랐던 것으로 기억한다. 사실 대형교회가 지역(local)에 관심을 두겠다는 것은 단순히 이웃 사랑의 미덕을 실천하려는 기독교적 윤리의 차원을 말하는 것이 아니다.

이웃하는 소규모 교회들과 동일한 방식으로 경쟁하듯 지역 전도에 집중하기보다는 대교회가 갖는 규모, 시너지, 인지성 등의 장점을 기반으로 더 넓은 지역과 지역교회들을 섬기는 방편이 되기를 원한 것이다. 그래서 건축사업도 단일 교회의 목표와는 차별화된 기독교 복합문화센터가 된 것이다. 그래서 건축이 단순-반복-거대의 유형을 벗어나 복합적이고 다양한 프로그램을 통해 다양-복합-풍부로 그 요소들이 효과적으로 분리되기도 하고 동시에 적극 섞여서 시너지를 드러내기 바라는 것이다.

Q. 이관석. 인간에게 땅은 어머니와 같은 존재다. 부모로부터 자식에게 물려지는 유전자가 모든 인간에게 내재된 것처럼 건축도 대지에서 추출된 특성을 담아내야 한다. 건축은 외부에서 보면 대지에 부가되는 것이지만 내부에서 보면 대지와 하나로 융합돼야 한다. BGVC의 땅은 이 교수님이 개념을 떠올리거나 구체화하는 데 어떤 영향을 미쳤나?

A. 이은석. 현 BGVC 대지는 원래 부산 사람들에게는 송월타올

Conversation.
신앙의 본질을 향한 건축적 형상화
an architectural manifestation of the essence of faith

200

이은석 × 이관석
Lee Eun-seok × Lee Kwan-seok

1

부지로 알려져 있어, 지금도 택시를 타고 옛 송월타올로 가자고 하면 그곳에 데려다준다. 오랫동안 대로변에 유일하게 비어 있던 부산 최후의 공지 같은 느낌을 주었던 땅이다. 또한 동래라는 부산 지역 내륙의 중심성과 온천천이라는 개천이 스쳐 지나가고, 지하철이 지상 전철로 바뀌는 지점이며, 동서남북으로부터 부산의 5갈래 도로가 모이는 접점이기도 했다. 거의 육각형에 가까운 대지 형태인 것도 바로 그러한 부산의 환경과 대응하는 태도인 것이다. 특히 대로와 온천천의 관계는 이 프로젝트를 풀어가는 근본적 출발점이었다.

부산의 중심을 가로지르는 대로와 1층 가로형 로비 홀이 대응하고, 주변의 자연 요소인 온천천과는 진입 광장과 건축물 전체를 감아 오르는 옥외 계단이 적극적으로 관계한다. 현상설계 현장설명회 때 이 땅을 방문했는데, 그때가 아직 추운 2월이었는데도 온천천변으로 수많은 시민들이 뛰거나 거니는 것을 보았다. 그 대지를 바라보며 많은 부산 시민들을 적극 초대하여 부전교회가 조성한 풍요를 함께 누리도록 하는 것은 여러 의미가 있을 것이라는 확신이 섰다. 그래서 교회 전체가 안식과 환대의 공간이 되었으며, 온천천에서 시작되어 광장과 공중마당과 여러 홀을 거쳐 휘감아 오르는 외부계단은 십자가 탑 아래 부산 전역을 전망하는 옥상정원에까지 도달한다. 그리고 도면을 펼쳐 하늘에서 내려다보는 땅의 형상은 그렇게 부산의 중심을 향해 미끄러지듯 진행하는 거대한 방주를 떠올리게 하였다.

Q. 이관석. 그 설명을 들으니 대지가 우리의 눈에 의해 감각과 지성 그리고 감성에 주어지는 자양분이자 건축의 토대임을 다시 한 번 실감하게 된다. 좋은 건축은 그것이 서 있는 자연 상태의 대지와 관계를 맺으며, 더 나아가 대지를 표현하고 있음을 보여준다. 그런 건축가의 의도가 각각의 상징성을 지닌 형태와 공간으로 BGVC에서 전개됐다.

특히 종교건축에서 상징성은 중요한 가치 중 하나일 것이다. 부전교회에서는 건축가의 의도와 그것이 구현된 건물의 형태와 공간 사이에 어떤 상징체계가 형성된 것이 느껴진다. 제대로 적용한 상징은 개념 전달을 위한 도구로서 사유와 존재 사이의 거리를 메워준다. 이 교수님은 교회 건축에서 상징적인 이미지조차도 기능적인 한 가치가 되어 건축되어야 한다고 했다. 이 교회에서 이런 상징들이 기능과 결합되고 공간적 의미까지 더해져 계획된 사례들을 말해 달라.

A. 이은석. 우선 건축의 들린 볼륨이 많은 사람들을 모으는 이 열린 교회의 미래지향적 가치를 상징적으로 가장 잘 보여주는 면이라고 생각한다. 또 1층을 중층으로 열어 내부를 관통하며 형성된 가로는 교회의 열린 철학을 지원하는 구체적 태도이며, 누구든지 교회의 내외부 공간을 드나들고 오르내리며 산책할 수 있는 평면 구성과 계단, 공간의 연속성과 단면적 상승감, 주변 도시와 적극 교감을 이루는 기능은 실제적으로 여는 행위이다. 이런 요인들이 결국 열린 교회의 가치를 실질적으로 풍요롭게 만들어준다고 믿는다.

첨탑 형상이나 감상적인 빛을 다루며 조형적 어휘만으로 드러나는 은유는 자칫 상징에만 머무를 한계가 있다. 하지만 개인과 공동체 모두에게 구체적인 개방성을 제공하는 건축 요소들은 우리 시대에 요구되는 교회의 살아있는 상징이라고 여긴다. 그리고 나는 개방적 프로그램을 지원하는 건축이야말로 미래 교회의 중대한 역할이라고 본다. 오늘날 교회의 열린 이미지는 열린 프로그램에서부터 비롯되며, 열린 프로그램은 또한 열린 건축으로부터 지원받게 되는 것이다. 부전글로컬비전센터는 일반적 교회의 예배실과 교육실 기능 이외에도 키즈 카페,

1 —— 동부교회, 내부가 훤히 들여다보이는 현대적 랜드마크
　　Dong-bu Church, transparent and modern landmark
2 —— 「새로운 교회건축, 이렇게 하라」, 이은석 저
　　「how to succeed in church construction」by Lee Eun-seok
3 —— 「프로테스탄티즘 윤리와 자본주의 정신」, 막스베버 저
　　「the protestant ethic and the spirit of capitalism」by Max Weber

2　　　　3

노인휴게공간, 도서관, 식당가, 웨딩홀, 음악 연주홀, 전시홀, 체육관과 스카이라운지 등을 완비하고 있다. 프로그램부터 이웃과 도시를 향해 한껏 열린 건축을 지향한 것이다.

Q. 이관석. **건축설계 행위를 여러 가지로 정의할 수 있겠지만 '개성의 보편화' 과정이라고도 할 수 있지 않을까 싶다. 건축가가 어떤 개념을 내세우고 그것을 실현시키기 위해 자신의 개성을 발현시키는데, 순수예술과 달리 건축에서는 이때 보편화 능력은 매우 중요하다. 이런 면에서 부전교회에서 상징은 눈길을 끄는 장식적 요소라기보다는 기능 및 공간과 건강하게 결합된 것에서 모더니즘의 합리성이 느껴진다.**

교수님의 작품에서 모더니즘은 변함없는 원칙으로 나타난다. 앞서 2000년대 들어 열린 예배와 열린 교회 정서의 확산을 시대적 특징으로 언급했는데, 부전교회의 큰 규모가 이 교회가 '열린 교회'가 돼야 할 필요성을 더욱 촉구한 것 같다. 이때의 열린다는 것은 교인들 간의 자유로운 교제 이상으로 교회를 다니지 않는 이웃에게 배려함을 뜻할 것이다. 성공 사례를 보기가 쉽지 않은데, 부전교회는 설계 개념부터 그랬고 교회가 열리고 환대해야 할 시대적 요청에 전적으로 반응한 것 같다. 그 시도가 성공적이었다고 여겨지나? 아쉬운 점이 있다면 어떤 것이 있을지?

A. 이은석. 교회의 건축적 컨셉은 획기적인 면이 적지 않으나, 사실 성공 여부는 건축적 결과물로만 얘기할 수 있는 것은 아니라고 생각한다. 건축가의 의도와 구체적 제시에도 불구하고 교회가 그렇게 사용하지 않으면 그러한 가치는 사라져 버린다. 입당을 한 올해, 내가 기대하던 만큼 부전교회 건축의 가치들이 전 영역에서 아직 새롭게 발휘되고 있지는 못하다는 생각이다.

무엇보다 광장의 활성화가 시급한데, 교회 전면에 가려져 있는 자동차 수리센터가 아직 철거되지 않았고, 도시와 온천천과 적극 연계되어야 하는 외부계단이 미완의 조경과 안전상의 문제로 인하여 그 연속의 파노라믹한 풍요를 잘 발휘하지 못하고 있다는 느낌이 있다. 열린 교회의 기능은 도시와 자연과 인간과의 연속성을 극대화하도록 경영하는 데 있다고 본다.

Q. 이관석. **프로그램의 사용윤리에 대한 중요한 지적으로 여겨진다. 좋은 교회당이 되려면 먼저 좋은 건축물이 돼야 한다. 이를 위해서는 건축가의 뛰어난 기량과 정성이 건축주의 열린 마음과 만나야 하고, 이후 계획 의도에 합당한 사용의 실천도 필수적이다. 부전교회 측에서도 중소 규모의 개별 교회 범주를 넘어선 복합적 프로그램을 지닌 채 기존 교회들과는 구별되는 접근법을 취한 대규모 교회당을 제대로 운영하는 데는 시간이 필요할 것이다.**

2010년대에 들어서 교회 건축의 특성으로 '추상성과 경건성 회복'이라는 새로운 상징 모색을 꼽으셨다. 이때의 경건성은 과거의 엄숙하거나 또는 화려하거나 거창해도 형식만 남은 예배를 위한 건축적 경건성을 뜻하지는 않을 것 같다. 교수님이 말씀한 경건성 회복은 무슨 의미인가?

A. 이은석. 약간 추상적인 면이기도 하지만, 현대 교회가 일차적인 실용성만을 목적으로 삼는 건조함에서 벗어나고, 대중성에 영합하며 세속적 공간의 활성화를 꾀하는 기름기만을 추구하기보다, 이 시대의 메마른 영성을 고조시키는 균형 있는 공간으로 거듭나기를 바라는 측면이다. 여기 교회 공간에 모여 지친 현대 도시민의 육신이 안식할 수 있고, 현대 사회와 거친 문화로 상처 입은 영혼들이 위로 받을 수 있는 공간을 조성하는 것은 오래되

Conversation.
신앙의 본질을 향한 건축적 형상화
an architectural manifestation of the essence of faith

202

이은석 × 이관석
Lee Eun-seok × Lee Kwan-seok

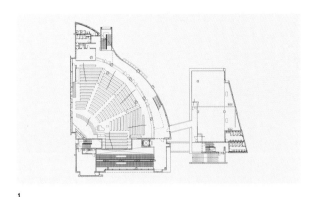

1

었지만 여전히 결핍된, 가까운 미래의 교회 건축이 우선적으로 회복해야 할 가치가 아니겠는가!

Q. 이관석. 말씀한 건축적 추상성은 건축의 기능을 가장 고양시킬 수 있는 방안이기도 하다. 추상성은 조직적이고 의식적이고 정신적인 현상으로서 무질서나 비조직화, 갈등 상황, 혼란을 극복하면서 기능을 아름다움의 원천으로 삼아 전면에 내세운다. 추상성을 새로운 상징으로 삼았다고 했는데 부전교회에서는 상징이 기능 및 공간성이 긴밀하게 연계되어 건강하다. 섣부른 상징으로 작위성을 풍기거나 별난 형태를 위한 변명으로 드러날 위험을 감소시켰다.

　　　이번에는 건축가, 건축주와 함께 성공적인 건축을 위해 삼위일체가 돼야 할 시공자에 대해 얘기해보자. 부전교회를 보면 높이 틀린 종탑과 캔틸레버, 엄청난 길이의 노출 콘크리트 외벽, 유연한 내부 공간성 등 구조와 재료, 형태와 공간 모두에서 난이도가 높은 작업이 수행됐다. 이런 작업이면 흔히 건축가와 시공자 사이에 갈등이 생기곤 하는데, 건축가 입장에서 볼 때 시공자의 자세는 어떠했나?

A. 이은석. 좋은 건축을 이루기 위해 설계자의 역할이 무엇보다 중요하겠지만, 만약 건축 작업에 참여하는 모두가 조화를 이루지 못하고 불협화음을 내면 건축물이 한순간에 졸작으로 전락해버린다는 것은 주지의 사실이다. 이번 프로젝트는 각 단계마다 여러 헌신적인 독지가들이 참여하여 더불어 성공을 거둔 결과물이다.

　　　가치가 높은 대지를 저렴한 비용으로 공동체가 제공받았을 뿐 아니라, 시공사가 결정되는 과정에서도 작품성에 대한 확신을 갖고 부산 지역을 대표하는 건설사가 지역 문화에 대

한 책임감을 갖고 파격적인 조건으로 기꺼이 동참하게 됐다. 나는 아직 그토록 진지한 열정으로 최고의 완성도에 도달하기 위해 전 공정에서 장인정신을 갖고 기술개발에 매진하는 시공사를 본 적이 없다. 이번 경우는 정말이지 작곡가보다 연주자에게 더욱 박수를 보내야 할 것 같다. 가슴을 졸이며 거푸집을 처음 떼어 냈을 때 빛을 발하며 깨질 듯한 도기처럼 반짝임으로 그 강성과 완벽성을 깔끔하게 드러내는 노출 콘크리트 품질에 감격했던 기억이 지금도 생생하다. 최고 폭 28미터, 전체 길이 458미터의 거대한 노출 콘크리트 벽면이 연속적으로 공중에서 흠결 없이 휘감아 오르게 하기 위해 시공사는 끊임없는 연구와 집중력, 각고의 노력을 기울였다. 적어도 한국에서는 보기 드문 고도의 기념적 노출 콘크리트 작업을 경동이라는 시공사가 이루어낸 것에는 누구도 이의를 달 수 없을 것이다. 이러한 여러 측면에서 봐도 부전교회가 더욱 이웃과 부산 지역을 위해 교회시설을 힘써 개방하고 함께 사용해야 할 책임감 같은 것을 느낄 만하다.

그런 시공사의 선의와 적극성을 만났다니 건축가에게는 고마운 일이다. 교회 건설현장에서 예산이 풍족하지는 않았을 텐데 시공사 대표뿐 아니고 현장의 실무 담당자들 모두의 정성이 없이는 불가능했을 것이다. 이번 경험을 통해 시공사의 시공능력도 상당히 향상됐을 것 같다. 부전교회에서 건축가와 건축주, 시공자 모두가 최선을 다해 만족스러운 결과를 얻은 흔치 않은 경우를 확인할 수 있었다. 퐁피두센터나 동대문디자인플라자처럼 이색적인 대규모 건물이 들어섰을 때에는 그 장소에 녹아드는 데 시간이 필요하기 마련이다. 부전교회가 처음의 지향점을 잃지 않고 열린 교회로서의 소임에 충실해 지역과 세계를 향해 빛과 소금의 역할을 다할 수 있기를 바란다.

An architectural manifestation of the essence of faith

Lee Eun-seok × Lee Kwan-seok

Q. LEE KWAN SEOK.　　　Congratulations on finishing the construction of Bujeon Presbyterian Church, a project you have been working on for a long time. What year did you first complete a church, from the designing stage to the building work, and how many churches have you built before we reach the Bujeon Presbyterian Church?

A. LEE EUN SEOK.　Looking over my records related to church architecture, my first church, the Mokyang church, was built in the year 2000 on a site of about 100-pyeong in Daejeon Yuseong. The beginning of a new millennium, the year 2000 was a very important year in my architectural career. I was selected in the design competition for the 'Millennium Gate', and I finished Mokyang Church, my first church project, that year. It was through these professional experiences that I began to confirm and confide my philosophy towards the 'minimum', which I still uphold as a precious value in my architectural design. I am not exactly sure of the precise number of churches that I have built thus far, but just from counting the number of new churches, I think that the number would be easily over 100.

Q. LEE KWAN SEOK.　　　Over the past 17 years, I think that you have designed and built the greatest number of churches of any architect in Korea, and perhaps even in the world. I don't think that this is a coincidence. What brought here and presented you with such an opportunity?

A. LEE EUN SEOK.　At the end of 20th century, the church architectural scene in Korea was seeking a new aesthetic represented by modernistic practicality and economic minimalism. The reason why opportunities to design church buildings came to me was, I think, because I began my architectural career with a modernistic spirit. Whether in terms of architecture, or in terms of a way of life, I am a full-time modernist. I grew up in a very pious protestant family governed by a very disciplined and Calvinistic way of life, which was almost puritan, and which was imposed on me. My studies abroad, when my architectural direction truly took shape, was teeming with the modernist examples in Paris, and with progressive and avant-garde philosophy. Although France is a catholic country, perhaps due to the fact that Calvin was born there, everything was progressive. Not just in society in general, but also culturally, French modern aesthetics somewhat went in line and thrived along with protestant philosophy. With this as my background, I came back to Korea in the late 1990s following this deep engagement with the modernistic architectural environments of Europe, and I found that while there were a large number of things to do with regards to church architecture, they were relatively postmodern and under an extreme aesthetic poverty, buried under formalism. Now when I look back, the building styles of churches such as Choonghyun Presbyterian Church in Gangnam, Kwanglim Methodist Church, the Daegu Jeil Church, and others seem somewhat comical to me, as I think that they misunderstood following — that the medieval gothic cathedral is the way to preserve faith and piety. At that time, Kyungdong Presbyterian Church, which

1 — 르 꼬르뷔지에의 롱샹교회
Notre-Dame du Haut Ronchamp by Le Corb
usier

2 — 인습적 교회 내부공간의
틀을 깬 롱샹교회
Notre-Dame du Haut Ronchamp, present a
new concept in the inner space of the chur
ch

1   2

is also a variant of a gothic cathedral, was built, and it also focused on the form. In this way, church architecture in Korea was conducted throughout the 1980s and 1990s in a state of ignorance and unpreparedness. In this situation, I merely made a conceptual suggestion towards a progressive and modern church architecture, and many churches and church leaders who were planning new buildings came to me unexpectedly in agreement and supported a modern church architect like me, who was not all that common at the time. At that time, I continued to write on new church architecture for the journal on ministry. I gathered them up and published them through Duranno under a book provocatively titled Act Like This for a New Church Architecture. I gave many talks on church architecture around the country, and I also remember being broadcast on radio and TV programmes related to church architecture.

Q. LEE KWAN SEOK. **I have attended many churches since my youth, and I have visited many examples of religious architecture both within and outside Korea, particularly as I began my studies in architecture. You mentioned something about Korean church architecture in the late 1990s – could you elaborate on this point a little further and share your thoughts on the changes made to protestant architecture after the modernization of Korea?**

A. LEE EUN SEOK. In the West, as the progressive Christian theological movement known as the ecumenical movement strove to unite all Christian churches across all denomi-

nations and differences, and a religious pluralism became commonplace, the church space was being used indiscriminately with no distinction drawn between the Catholics or the Protestants. However, I think that the reason why protestant practicality and aesthetic simplicity became so well known is due to the significant influence of the German sociologist Max Weber's The Protestant Ethic and the Spirit of Capitalism. Under the support of this philosophy, the common architectural aesthetic replaced a pious and sacred architecture. However, I think that Korean protestant churches began to think more seriously about architecture at a much later phase than other countries in the world. Personally, I think that the changes to the Korean protestant church began with the large-scale mass gathering named 'Explo 74' held in 1974 at Yeouido Plaza . After this period, the boundaries between different church denominations began to crumble, and the church began to develop confidence towards its mission in Korean society. During this period of revival, one can find traces of externalism and materialism, which can be found most distinctly in Korean church architecture. It seems that it is around this time that churches began to design balconies and fan-shaped planes in the main service halls. However, the fan-shaped form has a weak point, in that it tends to focus attention solely on the pastor. The existence of balcony seats also disrupts the church from forming a sense of solidarity during the service. More recently, we have witnessed a trend in which churches are beginning to slow down in terms of growth and are looking for a deeper connection to their services and the

Conversation.
신앙의 본질을 향한 건축적 형상화
an architectural manifestation of the essence of faith

206

이은석 × 이관석
Lee Eun-seok × Lee Kwan-seok

fellowship, and there is fortunately a growing inclination to build more single-floor churches with low-leveled, wide, and flat stages that support a united group consciousness.

Q. LEE KWAN SEOK.   **That kind of understanding of Korean Christian architecture must have led to the architecture of Bujeon Presbyterian Church today. Putting this aside for now, I would like to ask what you remember with the clarity when thinking about all of the religious buildings that you have seen thus far. It must have had influence on your planning in church architecture...**

A. LEE EUN SEOK.   As you might have guessed, the most memorable religious architecture to me is Le Corbusier's Notre Dame du Haut. Being a cathedral for catholic pilgrims, it may be difficult to find a direct connection between it and the function of a protestant church, but the fact that its architecture is liberated from that common gothic verticality and landmark character, and the fact that it has proposed a new religious architectural form drawn from an abstract aesthetic value, while also attempting to completely recreate tradition by making it difficult for it to be an example of my most memorable work of religious architecture. The tiny cross made out of metal beams and placed on top of the dome was especially shocking. Accustomed to general expectations in Korea, I was under the impression that a church is only a church when it has installed a cross in a provocative red neon light, regardless of whether it fits the outer appearance of the building or not. The feeling that I felt

at that moment was that it was so different from the reality of church architecture in Korea that the effect on me was like a vitamin injection. This effect was not in the size but in the contrasts. The various architectural positions of Le Corbusier were especially refreshing to me during my studies. Apart from this, I cannot but mention the La Tourette Monastery, which showcased the values of simplicity and humility, and the worth of an abstract space as demonstrated by its main service hall. Also, the Firminy Catholic Church, which was recently constructed after remaining for a long period as an unfinished project, was also impressive and a formative experience, even when I was already an middle aged architect. Fundamental experiments such as embracing form, space, and time in architecture were carried out there, and a completely new object that carries space, resembling something like a spaceship that humanity has never seen before, was also designed to reside there as well. While Brutalism and its values are being revisited again in recent academic discussion and in reference to phenomenology, as though such issues are bringing something new to the table, he had already made all these architectural advancements 50-60 years ago. It is a great help to us, the later architects who set foot on this earth, that such a great individual such as Le Corbusier had been here first.

Q. LEE KWAN SEOK.   **In terms of impressiveness, the lessons that the Notre Dame du Haut and the La Tourette Monastery offer, architectural highpoints, seem to exercise influence across time and space. You appear to understand**

1 —— 새로운 교회건축 유형의 가능성을 제시한 롱샹교회
        Notre-Dame du Haut Ronchamp, suggestion of new church building type
2 —— 첨탑을 축소하고 새로운 상징을 모색한 라투레트 수도원
        Monastery of Sainte Marie de la Tourette, look for a new symbol instead of a spire

2

the church as 'an architectural manifestation of the essence of faith'. Can you elaborate on the 'essence of faith for the protestant church', and how contemporary church architecture might pursue it?

A. LEE EUN SEOK.   From Mark's attic to the catacombs during the time of persecution, to the great cathedrals in the Medieval age and the sports gymnasiums of modern America, Christian communities have always needed a place to gather and worship. When Christians gather together for worship, they experience the God who resides among them. From this standpoint, I thought that the highest priority for church architecture is to shape the acts of opening and gathering in a physical space. While the ultimate aim in the Christian faith would be a formless church, in terms architecture one requires a certain value that can be manifested physically. These are the options encountered by all church architecture across generations, and which many have pondered: that is, how to create a gathering space that is also open. Hence, to pursue only a monumental effect or an ornamental form is not an approach for pursuing the essence in church architecture. Opening the doors to a mission, and allowing various paths to gather at one place for worship is at the core of church architecture, and the essential attitude required for church architecture. In Greek, the church is the ekklesia, that is, the people who are called out. As the gathering of people is a necessary element of a church, church architecture should make sure that this gathering function is efficiently fulfilled for the community to come together for worship.

Q. LEE KWAN SEOK.   By adopting the demands of contemporary culture, a church that protects, shares, and spreads its traditional and unchanging faith had to look for a new aesthetic, and this has brought about a very different result in terms of its architectural manifestations. From this view, what are your greatest concerns when observing at contemporary protestant architecture?

A. LEE EUN SEOK.   While it would be impossible to deny that symbolism is an essential part of architecture, when looking at the large, ostentatious crosses in the city and across the country, and when looking at the excessively monumental or uniquely shaped churches, it feels like the church is merely imitating a commercial signboard than discovering its true essence. It becomes like Robert Venturi's The Decorated Shed. Surely, there would be communities that cannot but accept such irregular church structures for various reasons, including financial demands in the knowledge that the situation is not ideal. However, when churches fall into such irregular definitions, despite having every means to avoid this, one cannot but think that too many churches in Korea have become too secularised and commercialised. They pour their attention into the outer appearance of architecture, and yet it is even more disheartening that they cannot assemble the outer appearance to a high standard.

Q. LEE KWAN SEOK.   This understanding of the

Conversation.

신앙의 본질을 향한 건축적 형상화
an architectural manifestation of the essence of faith

208

이은석 × 이관석
Lee Eun-seok × Lee Kwan-seok

need for the churches to overcome this problem must have become the background to your numerous church designs, and I think that this also applies to the Bujeon Presbyterian Church. Could you briefly explain your architectural concept that underlies the design of Bujeon Presbyterian Church?

A. LEE EUN SEOK.   If I was to make some suggestions for the countless churches in Korea that are still stuck in a superficial and formalist state, particularly regarding the necessary skills that will guide church design without fall-ing into the traps of formalism and symbolism, I would ask them to focus on emphasising the value of abstract space. Some of the values that I aimed to achieve when beginning the large-scale Bujeon Presbyterian Church project was firstly the symbol of the value of openness that is triggered by its elevated structure (a landmark of mission); secondly, the communication between the church, the city, and its neighbours, composed by the continuous flowing gesture made by the architecture (a landmark of love); and thirdly, the green garden and deck as a space of rest, which I tried to install wherever possible (a landmark of peace). These three spatio-conceptual aims became the core design concepts for Bujeon Presbyterian Church. I predict that these values will also apply to the churches that I will design in the future.

Q. LEE KWAN SEOK.   Various elements, including ministry direction and the singular vision of the Bujeon Presbyterian Church, the relationship between the earth including the site's conditions, the logical decisions made

to deal with the increased scale, and others, must have all been incorporated into that founding concept. What were your first impressions when you were introduced to the spatial programme and vision of the church's own ministry? Moreover, Bujeon Presbyterian Church is larger than any of the churches that you have dealt with in your career. Did you adopt a new approach either out of necessity or voluntarily, in order to deal with the difference in scale?

A. LEE EUN SEOK.   As you can observe from the project title, the Bujeon Presbyterian Church project began with a desire to become international and simultaneously region-al. The missionary attitude, to be open towards the world, is something most churches pursue with an equal degree of passion. However, the ministry direction of the church behind this construction was quite different. When a mega church expresses its desire to refocus its attention on the local inhabitants, it is not merely about practicing the virtue of neighbourly love at the level of a Christian ethical discourse. What it states instead is that it wishes to serve a wider region and the local churches, using the scale, syn-ergy, and influence of a mega church. Instead of focusing on smaller, local mission, as many neighbouring small-scale churches do in competition, the mega church widens its scope. This is why the project became a Christian cultural complex center, in contrast to what would be the more common aim for churches. This is why architecture goes over the naivety-repetition-enlargement pattern, and tries to not only effectively divide itself from those elements by

1 — 전위적 예배공간을 시도한 피르미니 교회
the Saint-Pierre church in Firminy, avant-garde space for worship

2 — 새로운 현대교회건축의 유형을 모색한 BGVC
BGVC, suggestion of contemporary church building type

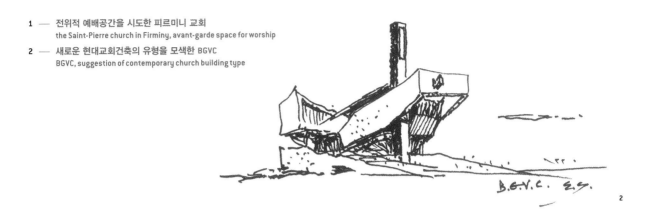

adopting complex and various programmes (via the pattern of variety-complexity-abundance) but also to incorporate them actively to arrive at a synergetic result.

Q. LEE KWAN SEOK. **The earth is like a mother to human beings. Just as the genes are passed down from one's parents to oneself, architecture too must be able to embrace the unique features captured on Earth. When looking from the outside, architecture appears to be something added to the earth, but when looking from the inside, architecture must be integrated with the earth. How did the site of the Bujeon Presbyterian Church influence your thought process and the manifestation phase?**

A. LEE EUN SEOK. The current site of the Bujeon Presbyterian Church used to be the site of the Songwol Towel for the Busan residents, and when one asks the cab driver to go to the old Songwol Towel site, he will still bring you there. It was a piece of land that remained empty for a long time by the main road, seemingly the final piece of empty land in Busan. Located at the centre of Busan, a river named Oncheoncheon flows by it, it marks the point where the subway goes above ground, and is also the connecting point where five roads in Busan from all directions meet. The reason why the plane takes on a hexagonal form is to deal with such conditions in Busan. Most particularly, the relationship between the main road and the Oncheoncheon was the fundamental starting point for this project. The horizontal first floor lobby hall reflects the main road outside, which

cuts across the centre of Busan, and the external staircase wraps around the plaza and the entire building to interact with its natural surrounding, such as the Oncheoncheon. I visited this place during the site orientation session for the design competition, and I saw that numerous citizens were out at the Oncheoncheon, despite the cold February weather. Looking at this scenery, I gained confidence that it would be meaningful for the Bujeon Presbyterian Church to invite all of those many Busan residents to share in a sense of abundance together. Hence, the entire church became a place of rest and hospitality, and the external staircase that begins at the Oncheoncheon cuts across and wraps around the plaza, the raised yard, and various halls, and arrives at the rooftop garden under the cross where one can enjoy the entire view of Busan. Furthermore, when looking over the blueprint, the shape of the land from a top-down view evoked the idea of an enormous ark sliding down towards the centre of Busan.

Q. LEE KWAN SEOK. **Upon listening to that explanation, I am reminded again of how the land provides the main ingredients for the eyes in terms of perception, cognition, and emotion, and even function as the basis for architecture. Good architecture forms a relationship with the land in its natural state, and goes further to express it. Such architectural intentions can be observed in Bujeon Presbyterian Church in terms of its form and space, which carry its own respective symbolic meanings. Symbolism is one of the most important values for the built environment,**

Conversation.

신앙의 본질을 향한 건축적 형상화
an architectural manifestation of the essence of faith

210

이은석 × 이관석
Lee Eun-seok × Lee Kwan-seok

especially in religious architecture. In Bujeon Presbyterian Church, I can feel that there is a certain symbolic system installed between the intention of the architect and the form and space of the manifested building. A properly applied symbol fills up the gap between thought and existence, as an idea-conveying instrument. You mentioned that even a symbolic image must also be a functional value in church architecture. Could you give some examples of those functions that have integrated with such symbols and have a spatial meaning added to them?

A. LEE EUN SEOK.   First of all, I think that the elevated volume of the architecture reveals most vividly the future-oriented symbolic value of the open and welcoming church. The horizontality that cuts across the interior, by opening up the first floor to the middle floor, embodies specific and supportive attitudes towards the open ministry of the church. The plane composition and the staircase allows anyone to enter and walk around the interior and exterior space of the church; the continuity of the staircase and the cross-sectional elevation, and the function of encouraging the formation of connections with the surrounding city are all dynamic acts that open the church to the public. I believe that these elements enrich the value of this open church. The metaphor of the spire top and the ornamental vocabulary achieved in the sentimental lighting reaches the limits of remaining a symbol. However, I think that the architectural elements that provide a sense of openness to an individual and to the community become the living symbol of a church,

and a spiritual space that is demanded by this era. Also, I think that the primary role of architecture now is to support an open programme which will lead to future churches. The open image of the church today is based on the open programme, and the open programme is supported by open architecture in turn. The Bujeon Glocal Vision Center holds not only the main service hall and the staff rooms, as found in most churches, but also a kids café, a resting lounge for the elderly, a library, a food court, a wedding hall, a concert hall, an exhibition hall, a sports hall, a sky lounge, and other multipurpose spaces. From its programme, it strives to be an architecture that is truly open to the neighbour and the city.

Q. LEE KWAN SEOK.   The act of architectural design can be defined in many ways, but I wonder if it could be known as part of the procedure of 'generalising one's unique character'. An architect may come forward with a certain concept and try to realise it via one's own unique style, but, unlike the fine arts, it is also important to generalize in architecture as well. In that respect, the symbol of Bujeon Presbyterian Church seems to convey the rationality of modernism from its sound integration of function and space, rather than in its ornamental effects. In your works, modernism appears to be an unchanging principle. Earlier you mentioned the phenomenon of open service and the expansion of an open church as an era-specific feature from the 2000s onwards, and I think that the largesse of Bujeon Presbyterian Church acted as a catalyst in provoking this

Conversation.
신앙의 본질을 향한 건축적 형상화
an architectural manifestation of the essence of faith

212

이은석 × 이관석
Lee Eun-seok × Lee Kwan-seok

1

2

need for an 'open church'. I understood this openness to mean going beyond fellowship among church members, and to show hospitality towards neighbours who are not members of the church. It is difficult to find successful cases, but Bujeon Presbyterian Church seems to have responded fully to the call for an open and a hospitable church from its concept planning stages. Do you think that this attempt has succeeded? If you are aware of any possible improvements, what are they?

A. LEE EUN SEOK.   While there are quite a number of revolutionary elements within the architectural concept of the church, I think that its success cannot be evaluated solely from the architectural result itself. If the church does not use the building in the way the architect intended or specifically suggested, then its value disappears. Having opened this year, I feel that the architectural values of Bujeon Presbyterian Church are not being fully realised in all areas as I expected. The use of the plaza is of the highest priority, but the car repair centre that covers the front of the church has not yet been demolished, and the external staircase that must connect the church to the city. Oncheoncheon does not realise its panoramic plenitude from its element of continuity due to the unfinished landscape and its safety concerns. I think that an open church functions best when it is managed in such a way as to maximise the continuity between city, nature, and man.

Q. LEE KWAN SEOK.   This could be perceived as an

important critique on the ethical use of the programme. To be a good church, it first has to be good architecture. For thist, the great skill of an architect needs to come in connection with the open mind of the building owner, and then the practice that is appropriate to the agreed planning intentions must necessarily follow. But, looking from the Bujeon Presbyterian Church's view, more time is required to properly manage a large-scale church that has an approach that is quite distinct from the other mega churches in the area, equipped with their own complex programmes. In 2010, you picked 'Abstractness and Restoration of Devoutness' as a new symbolic direction that represents the unique features of church architecture. I think that the devout element here does not merely mean the solemnity of the past or an architectural devotion that is geared towards a merely formalistic worship in an ostentatious building. What do you mean exactly by the restoration of devoutness?

A. LEE EUN SEOK.   This may sound a little abstract, but it is my desire that contemporary churches will step out from this stalemate where they look at everything from a utilitarian approach and develop this approach to become a space in which a balance can revitalize the dull spirituality of this age, instead of merely seeking to utilise the vitality of a secularized space by incorporating mass culture. isn't it of the highest priority that this old and yet debilitated church architecture of the near future be restored and built a space where souls that have been hurt by this contemporary age and its brutality can come to

1 — 둘린 볼륨으로 열린 가치를
획득하려는 의도의 개념
concept of intention to obtain
open value with lifted volume

2 — 도시를 향해 열려 있는
옥외계단의 효과
effect of outdoor stairs that is
open towards the city

3 — 사랑의 랜드마크 개념도
diagram, landmark for love

4 — 평화의 랜드마크 개념도
diagram, landmark for peace

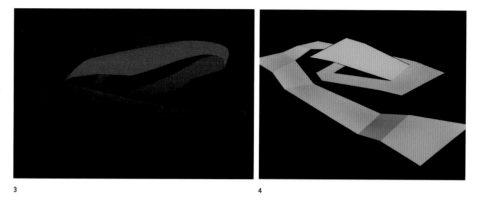

3

4

receive some kind of consolation?

Q. LEE KWAN SEOK.　　　Architectural abstraction is one of the methods thought to truly enhance the function of architecture. As a systematic, conscious, and psychological phenomenon, abstraction can overcome disorderliness, conflict situations, and chaos, and put forward the function of architecture as the foundation of beauty. You said that you chose abstraction as the new symbol – and it seems that the symbol is functioning well as it is tightly connected to function and spatiality in the Bujeon Presbyterian Church. It reduced the risk of seeing like an excuse for a strange form or risking looking ostentatious as a mere shallow symbol. Let us now talk about the construction company, who forms a trinity with the architect and the building's owner for a successful construction. When we look at the Bujeon Presbyterian Church, it has a highly-elevated bell tower and cantilever, an exposed concrete wall of great length, a flexible interior spatiality, and others – it was a work of high difficulty whether in terms of structure, material, form, or space. There tends to be conflict between the architect and the construction party in this kind of projects. How cooperative was the construction company from your point of view as an architect?

A. LEE EUN SEOK.　The role of the designer is probably the most important for good architecture, but it is also a fact that architecture can fail if the participating parties all corroborate in their wish to cooperate and alleviate discord between each other. This project demonstrates a result that could only succeed through the numerous contributions of dedicated benefactors at every stage. Not only was the community provided with expensive land at an affordable price, a construction company that represents the Busan region in terms of quality of labour – to bear the responsibility towards their regional culture – emerged enthusiastic to participate in the construction under exceptionally generous conditions during the decision-making phase. Until then, I have never met a construction company that strove as hard and with such a sincere, passionate, and professional attitude towards technical development across all phases in order to produce the best results. In this case, I feel that applause should go to the player instead of the composer. I still remember clearly that moment of awe when I was waiting in high expectation as the exposed concrete had its cast removed, revealing a shiny and ceramic-like high-quality exposed concrete that was strong, immaculate, and impressive. In order to make the 458m-long, 28m-wide exposed concrete wall to continuously spin upwards flawlessly in midair, the construction company had to devote themselves to endless research, focus, and extreme hard effort. No one will be able to question that this construction company, named Kyungdong, had completed this highly monumental exposed concrete work, which is still rare in Korea. When looking over these various aspects, it feels normal that Bujeon Presbyterian Church would feel the burden of responsibility to open and share the church facilities amongst its neighbours and throughout the Busan region.

Conversation.
신앙의 본질을 향한 건축적 형상화
an architectural manifestation of the essence of faith

214

이은석 × 이관석
Lee Eun-seok × Lee Kwan-seok

It is fortunate that you encountered such good will and enthusiasm from the construction company. The funding must not have been plentiful at the church construction site, and the project would not have been possible without dedication from not only the representative of the construction company but also from all of the people in charge at the site. I expect that the construction skills of the construction company have also greatly improved throughout this experience. In Bujeon Presbyterian Church, I was able to witness a rare occasion in which the architect, the building owner, and the construction company all put in their best efforts to achieve a satisfactory result. When a unique large-scale building such as the Pompidou Center or the Dongdaemun Design Plaza is set in place, time is necessary for the building to assimilate itself in the location. I hope that Bujeon Presbyterian Church will not lose sight of its earliest intentions and function faithfully in connection to its calling as an open church, ultimately fulfilling its role as the light and salt of the world and the region.

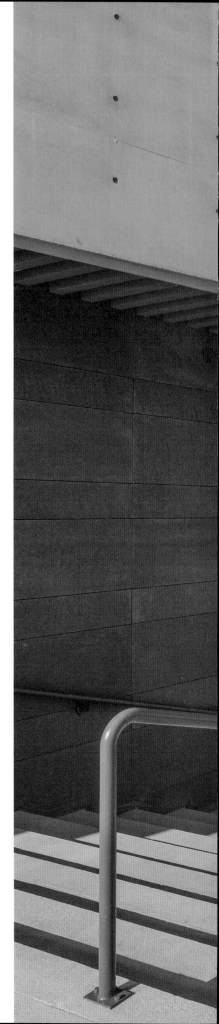

열어라
마음을, 세상을, 하늘을

김혁준
픽셀하우스 편집장

우연히 카페 문 앞에 걸린 'OPEN' 팻말을 보았다. 늘 지나치던 일상의 메시지. 뒷면에 적힌 'CLOSED'를 보고 발길을 돌렸던 기억이 있다면 'OPEN'은 매우 반가운 인사다. 문득 이 단어의 의미가 궁금해졌다. 쉬운 단어이기에 한 번도 사전을 찾아본 적이 없던 말. OPEN을 찾기 위해 책을 펼쳤다.

OPEN.

1. Not Closed: 열려 있는, 떠져 있는, 펼쳐진, 막혀 있지 않은
2. Not Fastened: (묶거나 덮지 않고) 열어 놓은, 잠기지 않은
3. Not Enclosed: (사방이) 막혀 (둘러싸여) 있지 않은, 툭 트인
4. Not Covered: (덮개/지붕)이 없는; 옥외(노천)의
5. Not Hidden: 개방된, 누구나 아는, 공개된, 숨김없는, 솔직한
6. Not Restricted: (시합 등이) 공개되어 있는, 누구나 참여할 수 있는, 누구나 이용(사용)할 수 있는
7. Not Yet Dediced: 아직 확정되지 않은

이상하게 들리겠지만 열려 있다는 건, 닫혀 있지 않다는 뜻이다. 긍정의 가치를 설명하기 위해서 강한 부정을 사용해야 하는 특별한 경우다. OPEN은 우리가 한정지었던 테두리를 벗어나 경계를 사라지게 하는 것이다. 정해진 것으로부터 자유롭지 못하면 결코 만들어 낼 수 없는 지향점을 가리키고 있다.

부전글로컬비전센터를 설명하는 데 이보다 좋은 말을 찾지 못했다. 아주 쉽고 단순하지만 그 의미를 지키기 위해서는 매 순간 부단한 노력이 필요한 말이다. 그리고 앞으로 이 집이 이 땅에서 해야 할 일에 대해서도, 살아가야 할 우리의 모습에도 분명 의미 있는 열쇠가 되어 줄 것이다. 우리의 마음을 열고, 삶을 열고, 하늘을 바라보자.

Open up your Mind to the World and to the Sky

Kim Hyouk-joon Director, Pixelhouse

I accidentally saw the 'OPEN' sign in front of the cafe door. Always a routine message. If there is a memory that I looked back at 'CLOSED' on the back, 'OPEN' is a very nice greeting. I suddenly became curious about the meaning of this word. A word that has never been found in the dictionary because it is an easy word. I opened my book to find OPEN.

OPEN. very important vocabulary

1. **Not Closed**: unfolded, unobstructed
2. Not Fastened: unlocked(unbundled)
3. Not Enclosed: tuck-in, which is not blocked(surrounded)
4. Not Covered: without cover; Outdoor(open-air)
5. Not Hidden: open-minded, frank
6. Not Restricted: Anyone who is open to the public
7. Not Yet Decided: Not yet confirmed

This is going to sound silly , but being open means that it is not closed. It is a special case in which a strong denial must be used to account for the value of affirmation. OPEN is to make the boundaries disappear beyond the boundaries we have made. If you are not free from what you have set, it points to an orientation that you can never create.

I could not find a better word to describe the local vision center. It is very easy and simple, but it requires constant effort every moment to keep its meaning. And it will surely be a meaningful key for what we have to do in this land and for our future to live.

부전교회   Bujeon Presbyterian Church

History

감사하고 화목하고 충성하여 하나님을 영화롭게 하자!
Glory to God with thankfulness, fellowship, and stewardship!

예수님의 제자되어 부산과 민족과 세계에 축복의 통로가 되는 공동체
Equipped as disciples of Jesus, a community blessing Busan,
Nation, and the world

1932. 03. 05	부산진교회 서면기도소로 출발
	started the Seomyun chapel of Busanjin Church
1934. 12. 30	부산진교회에서 분립하여 부전교회로 개칭
	separated from Busanjin Church,
	renamed Bujeon Presbyterian Church
1945. 08. 15	경남 노동훈련소로 교회당 이전
	moved church to Gyeongnam Labor Training Center
1950. 12	천막교회 시작
	started the tent church
1952. 06. 01	성전 완공
	completed the church
1960. 08	성전 증축
	extended the church
1975. 11. 13	새 성전 봉헌식
	held a new building dedication ceremony
1996. 03. 22	교육관, 주차장 준공
	completed the educational center and parking lot
2001. 11. 07	교육관, 기도원, 주차장 준공
	completed the educational center,
	prayer center and parking lot
2002. 03. 03	교회설립 70주년 기념예배
	70th anniversary worship
2007. 02. 24	헤세드 학사관 개관
	opened 'Chesed' dormitory
2007. 06. 10	제1차 리모델링 완공
	completed renovation(the first construction)
2011. 01. 13	부전글로컬비전센터 현상설계 공모
	Architectural Design Competition for BGVC

2011. 04. 25	현상설계경기 당선작 발표(당선작: ㈜코마 건축사사무소)
	Announcement of Architectural Design Competition
	Winners: Atelier KOMA
2012. 01. 08	부전글로컬비전센터 건축설계계약
	made a contract with Atelier KOMA
2012. 03. 04	교회설립 80주년 감사예배
	80th anniversary worship
2012. 09. 28	부전글로컬비전센터 건축허가 승인
	got permission for architectural design
2012. 03. 04	교회설립 80주년 감사예배
	hold a building dedication ceremony
2012. 09. 28	부전글로컬비전센터 건축허가 승인
	got permission for architectural design
2013. 08. 23	부전글로컬비전센터 시공사 계약
	made a contract with Kyungdong Construction Co. Ltd.
2013. 08. 25	부전글로컬비전센터 착공예배
	Groundbreaking worship of BGVC
2016. 12. 24	부전글로컬비전센터 입당 예배
	dedication of BGVC

Designed by Atelier KOMA

BJGV

부전교회
BUJEON PRESBYTERIAN CHURCH

Bujeon
Website

아뜰리에 코마 + 이은석

Atelier KOMA + Lee Eun-seok

History

1995.	- KOMA 국제현상설계 당선, 아뜰리에 KOMA 오픈 Won at KOMA(Korean American Museum of Art and Cultural Center, Los Angeles) International Design Competition, the reason of opening atelier KOMA
1998.	- 문화공간 탑정(논산) Tapjung Luce
2000.	- '천년의 문' 현상설계 당선(서울) Millennium Gate - 목양교회(유성) Mokyang Church
2002.	세계비전교회(용인, 2003 경기도 건축문화상_금상) World Vision Church
2003.	- 경산교회(경산, 대한민국 건축문화 대상_우수상) Kyung San Church - 꿈의 학교 기숙사(서산) Dream School Dormitory
2004.	- 명지교회(서산) Myungji Church
2005.	- 사월교회(대구) Sawol Church
2006.	- 푸른마을교회(포항) Green Village Church - 동부교회(풍기) Dongbu Church - 근생시설 '우전가'(서울, 2006 강남구 아름다운 건축상) UJeon Ga
2007.	- 아간코리아 사옥 '뱅루즈'(과천) Vin Rouge
2009.	- 리안 하우스(광주, 경기도 건축문화상 동상) Lyann House - 범어교회(대구, 대구시 건축상 은상, 국민일보 교회건축 대상) Pomo Church
2010.	- 늘샘교회(광명, 경기도 건축문화상 은상) Neul Sem Church - 새문안교회 현상설계 당선(서울) Saemoonan Church
2011.	- 기쁨의 교회(광주) Joyful Church
2012.	- 총신대 사당캠퍼스 신관(서울, 서울시건축상 우수상) Chonshin University
2014.	- 하늘보석교회(서산, 한국건축가협회상) Heavenly Gem Church
2015.	- 성광교회(대전) Holy Light Church
2016.	- 애국지사 손양원 기념관(함안, 한국문화공간상 뮤지엄부문) Son Yang Won Memorial Museum, KICA Cultural Space Awards - 관광호텔 엔트라(서울) Hotel Entra
2017.	- 부전글로컬비전센터(부산, 2017 부산다운 건축상_금상) Bujeon Glocal Vision Center

Publication

2001.	「새로운 교회건축 이렇게 하라」, 두란노 「How to Succeed in Church Construction」, Duranno
2005.	「미완의 근대성」, 경희대 출판국 펴냄 「Unfinished modernity」, Kyung Hee University Press
2007.	「건축가, 이은석」, 건축세계 펴냄 「Pro Architect, LEE EUNSEOK」, Archiworld Publisher
2008.	「아름다운 교회 건축」, 두란노 「Beautiful Church Architecture」, Duranno

Exhibition

2007.	건축가 이은석, 현대 교회건축 및 문화 건축(과천) 「Modern church architecture and cultural architecture」
2014.	Point-Counterpoint, Trajectories of Ten Korean Architects, Paris
2015.	여기, 이어지다 : 한. 프 건축전, 김중업 박물관 Ici, Continuer

 Atelier KOMA
Website

경동건설주식회사

Kyungdong Construction Co., Ltd.

History

1973. 11. 12	경동건설㈜ 설립
	established Kyungdong Construction Co., Ltd.
1979. 12. 13	토목건축공사업 면허 취득
	License acquisition, Engineering and Construction
1987. 03. 31	주택건설사업자 등록
	registration, housing construction business operator
2000. 08. 12	본사사옥 건립, 이전
	construction of office building, relocate an office
2006. 08. 21	부산광역시 향토기업 선정
	selected local company by Busansi
2010. 02. 24	부산광역시 우수기업인 선정
	selected Business Award by Busansi
2013. 06. 18	건설의 날 은탑산업훈장 수훈
	received Presidential Citation of Silver Medal Order of Industrial Service
2015. 10. 29	대한건축학회 창립 70주년기념 공로상
	received Achievement Award, Architectural Institute of Korea
2017. 09. 01	부전글로컬비전센터, 부산다운건축상 금상 수상
	received Busan Architecture Award(Gold Medal), BGVC

Major project achievements

- 창원 국가공업기지 차룡단지 조성
  Changwon National Industrial Cheongryong Complex
- 거제아주지구 도시개발사업
  Geoje-Aju district Urban Development Project
- 해운대 경동제이드
  Haeundae Kyungdong Jade
- 장유 경동리인 하이스트
  Jangyu Kyungdong LEEIN Highest
- 문현 경동리인
  Munhyun Kyungdong LEEIN
- 토성 경동리인타워
  Tosung Kyungdong LEEIN Tower
- 신라대학교 캠퍼스 조성
  Silla Univ. Campus
- 동서대학교 센텀시티R&D타운
  Dongseo Univ. Centumcity R&D Town
- 부산시 교육위원회 청사
  Busan Metropolitan City Office of Education
- 한국해양수산개발원
  Korea Maritime Institute(KMI)
- 동아대학교 부민캠퍼스 종합강의동
  Dong-A Uni. Bumin Campus Multipurpose Academic Building

 Kyungdong Construction Co., Ltd.
Website

부전글로컬비전센터

위치	부산광역시 동래구 중앙대로 1276
용도	종교시설, 근린생활시설, 사회시설, 교육연구시설
대지면적	7,832.00 m^2
건축면적	4,675.00 m^2
연면적	42,404.74 m^2
규모	B5, 10F
구조	철근콘크리트, 철골
외부마감	노출 콘크리트
내부마감	노출 콘크리트, 화강석, 페인트
설계기간	2012. 1 - 2013. 5
공사기간	2013. 8 - 2017. 5
건축가	이은석(경희대학교)
건축설계	아뜰리에 코마 + 희림건축
구조설계	(주)유진구조이앤씨
기계	주성엔지니어링
전기	한길엔지니어링
시공	경동건설주식회사
사진	윤준환

Bujeon Glocal Vision Center

Location	1276, Jungang-daero, Dongnae-gu, Busan, Republic of Korea
Use	Church, Neighborhood Living Facilities, Social facilities, Education & Research facilites
Site Area	7,832.00 m^2
Building Area	4,675.00 m^2
Total Floor area	42,404.74 m^2
Building Scope	B5, 10F
Structure	Reinforced concrete, Steel frame
Exterior Finish	Euro-form exposed concrete
Interior Finish	Euro-form exposed concrete, Granite stone, Paint
Design period	2012. 1 - 2013. 5
Construction period	2013. 8 - 2017. 5
Project Architect	Lee Eun-seok (Kyung Hee Univ.)
Design team	Atelier KOMA + Heerim Architects & Planners Co., Ltd.
Structural engineer	Yujin Structural Engineering Construction CO., Ltd.
Mechanical engineer	Jusung Eng CO., Ltd.
Electrical engineer	Hangil Engineering CO., Ltd.
Construction	Kyungdong Construction Co., Ltd.
Photography	Yoon Joon-hwan

참여자

Participants

부전교회 건축위원회
Bujeon Presbyterian Church

박성규 Park Sung-kyu
백홍기 Paik Hong-ki
조강래 Cho Kang-rae
최영철 Choi Young-chul
조관기 Cho Kwan-ki
최창근 Choi Chang-keun
조성호 Cho Sung-ho
이석원 Lee Suck-won

경동건설
Kyungdong Construction Co. Ltd.

김재진 Kim Jae-jin
김정기 Kim Jung-ki
손봉익 Son Bong-ik
송경수 Song Gyeong-su
노경철 No Gyeong-cheol
김종호 Kim Jong-ho
이병주 Lee Byeung-joo

아뜰리에 코마
Atelier KOMA

이은석 Lee Eun-seok
안옥순 An Ok-soon
백진기 Baek Jin-kee
신인호 Shin Iin-ho
전창배 Jeon Chang-bae
김용현 Kim Yong-hyun
황정현 Hwang Jung-hyun
김성훈 Kim Sung-hun
김동일 Kim Dong-il
오지훈 Oh Ji-hoon
정준용 Jung Jun-yong
이우석 Lee Woo-seok
유지연 Yoo Jee-yeon
김소연 Kim So-yeon

희림건축사사무소
Heerim Architects & Planners

이승우 Lee Seung-woo

세움건축사사무소
Seum Architects

박현옥 Park Hyun-ok

(주)한국건설환경연구원
Korea Construction Environment Research

장성두 Jang Sung-do

(주)유진구조이엔씨
Yujin Engineering & Construction Co. Ltd

유진오 Yoo Jin-oh

(주)주성이엔지
JUSUNGENG Co. Ltd

권병인 Kwon Byong-in

(주)한길이엔지
Hangil Engneering Co. Ltd

조생수 Cho Saning-su

(주)모티브
Motive

김유천 Kim Yu-chon
정환황 Jeong Hwan-wang

1쇄 펴냄	2018년 3월 3일
지음	이은석
사진	윤준환
기획	부전교회
	경동건설주식회사
	아뜰리에 코마
자문	박성규, 김재진, 김정기
협력	조성호, 손봉익, 안옥순, 최상동
편집	김혁준
디자인	그래픽바이러스
번역	월간 「공간」
교정	스토리디자인
제작	픽셀커뮤니케이션

Writer	Lee Eun-seok
Photo	Yoon Joon-hwan
Planning	Bujeon Presbyterian Church
	Kyungdong Construction Co., Ltd.
	Atelier KOMA
Advice	Park Sung-kyu, Kim Jae-jin, Kim Jung-ki
Support	Cho Sung-ho, An Ok-soon, Son Bong-ik , Choi Sang-dong
Editing	Kim Hyouk-joon
Design	Graphicvirus
Translation	SPACE Magazine
proofreader	Story Design
Production	Pixelcommunication

펴낸이	이정해
펴낸곳	픽셀하우스
등록	2006년 1월 20일 제319-2006-1호
주소	서울시 동작구 신대방2동 364-140, 202호

Published by Pixelhouse
rm 202, 44, Yeouidaebang-ro 22ma-gil, Dongjak-gu, Seoul, Republic of Korea
tel +81 (2) 825 3633, fax +81 (2) 2179 9911
www.pixelhouse.co.kr
pixelhouse@naver.com

ISBN 978-89-98940-09-6 03610
40,000won

printed in republic of korea